25 Puppet Plays About Bible People

by Margaret Cheasebro

Library of Congress Cataloging-in-Publication Data

Cheasebro, Margaret, 1945-
25 puppet plays about Bible people / by Margaret Cheasebro.
p. cm.
Summary: A collection of twenty-five puppet plays presenting various Bible occupations so that the audience may guess which Bible character is being depicted. Includes instructions for making puppets and building a puppet stage.
ISBN 0-87403-852-9
1. Puppet plays, American. 2. Bible plays, American. 3. Puppet theater in Christian education. 4. Puppet making. [1. Puppet plays. 2. Bible plays. 3. Puppet making. 4. Puppet theater.]
I. Title. II. Title: Twenty-five puppet plays about Bible people.
PN1970.C44 1991
812'.54--dc20 91-7578
CIP
AC

Table of Contents

Wag Those Wooly Tails (*Shepherd*) 5
Have Hammer, Will Build (*Carpenter*) 9
Building Better Business (*Builders*) 12
Get Me A Seamstress—Quick! (*Seamstress*) 16
Fair's Fair (*Judge*) 18
Sample the Fare (*Cupbearer*) 20
There's A Crack in Your Crystal Ball (*Sorcerer*) 23
I Spy (*Spy*) 26
Open Wide, Say Ahhh (*Doctor*) 28
Let the Music Ring (*Musician*) 30
Harvest Time (*Farmer*) 32
Roll That Dough (*Baker*) 35
Pay Up, Buddy (*Tax collector*) 37
Learn Your ABCs (*Teacher*) 39
Polish That Silver (*Silversmith*) 41
This Is the House That God Built (*Craftsman*) 44
Lock 'Em Up! (*Jailer*) 47
The Grape Juice Stand (*Vintner*) 49
Bait That Line (*Fishermen*) 51
Make Room for More (*Innkeeper*) 53
How Good Is Your Shorthand? (*Secretary*) 56
March in Step (*Soldier*) 61
I Do Windows (*Personal servant*) 64
Playing Politics (*Politician*) 66
Under the Big Top (*Tent maker*) 70
How to Make Puppets 73
How to Build a Puppet Stage 78

Wag Those Wooly Tails

Characters:

- **Yousef**
- **Ahmed**
- **Abraham**
- **Isaac**
- **Jacob**
- **Moses**
- **David**
- **Amos**
- **Jesus**

(Abraham, Isaac, Jacob, Moses, David, Amos and Jesus can be the same puppet with a different-colored head piece, and/or different costumes.)

Yousef: Good morning, Ahmed.

Ahmed: Hello, Yousef. Ready for another day of work at the Bethlehem Employment Agency?

Yousef: Yes. Today we're interviewing shepherds. The Bethel Wool Company needs five more of them.

Ahmed: I saw several fellows out in the hall who look as though they might have had some experience. Shall we get started?

Yousef: Yes. The first one's name is Abraham. Call him in.

(*Ahmed goes to the side, calls, Abraham enters.*)

Ahmed: Uhh... excuse me, old timer, are you here about a shepherd's job?

Abraham: Yes.

Yousef: Pardon me for saying so, Abraham, but you look a little old for this job. Are you sure you can handle it?

Abraham: I've spent most of my life looking after sheep, goats and other animals. I can do it.

Yousef: So you're experienced?

Abraham: Very. I have owned thousands of sheep in my time.

Yousef: Then why are you interested in taking care of someone else's animals?

Abraham: To keep me humble. I am a rich man in charge of many people and animals. Sometimes I forget what it's like to be a simple sheepherder. So every now and then I remind myself by working for someone else.

Yousef: That's a most unusual attitude.

Abraham: It pays to give things up when God tells you to.

Yousef: God tells you to give things up?

Abraham: Sometimes.

Yousef: What things have you given up?

Abraham: Once God told me to leave my home in Ur and travel to a strange place. He didn't tell me where I was going, but I gave up my home to obey Him, and I've never been sorry that I did.

Yousef: I see. So you are looking for temporary work?

Abraham: Yes, sir.

Ahmed (*to Yousef*): He sounds a little senile. No one who can think straight would leave a life of luxury to be a sheepherder, even for a little while.

Yousef (*to Abraham*): Thank you very much. We'll tell you later if you got the job.

(*Abraham exits.*)

Ahmed: Next.

(*Isaac enters.*)

Yousef: What's your name?

Isaac: Isaac.

Yousef: Why do you want this job?

Isaac: I have something to offer besides experience, sir. You see, I've been around a lot of sheepherders, and I know they can be pretty rowdy—especially when they get into disputes at water wells. I'm good at settling arguments.

Yousef: What method do you use?

Isaac: I stay calm. I never fight. And if I have to, I leave to find another well.

Yousef: You mean you give up?

Isaac: Only if I have to. I'm pretty good at talking people into doing the right thing. They know I'm a peaceful man.

Yousef: It can be a long distance between wells. Have any sheep died because you didn't fight for your right to use a well?

Isaac: No, I've never lost a sheep that way.

Ahmed (*to Yousef*): He sounds like a coward, always running from a fight. We need someone more aggressive.

Yousef (*nods to Ahmed, turns to Isaac*): Thank you very much. We'll tell you later if you got the job.

(*Isaac exits.*)

Ahmed: Next.

(*Jacob enters.*)

Yousef: What's your name?

Jacob: Jacob.

Yousef: How much experience have you had?

Jacob: Let's see. I herded my father-in-law's sheep for twenty years, and then I got flocks of my own.

Yousef: What is a shepherd's main task?

Jacob: To increase the herd and improve the stock. I'm very good at that. I have a special technique that can produce spotted sheep or plain-colored sheep, and I know how to breed stronger, healthier animals.

Ahmed (*to Yousef*): This one could be a swindler.

Yousef: Thank you very much. We'll tell you later if you got the job.

Jacob (*as he exits*): Don't forget; I'm an expert.

Ahmed: Next.

(*Moses enters.*)

Yousef: What's your name?

Moses: Moses.

Yousef: How many years of experience have you had as a shepherd?

Moses: Let's see. I herded sheep and goats for forty years. Then I herded people for another forty years—herding people is much harder.

Ahmed (*to Yousef*): This one's a real smart aleck.

Yousef: Tell me, what is a shepherd's main job?

Moses: To make sure the sheep get proper care and food, and to see that they all return to the sheepfold at night.

Yousef: Are those your same goals when you, uh, herd people?

Moses: Yes, but with people you have to be more watchful. They're much harder to please, you can't trust them, and they're always getting into fights.

Yousef: Where did you herd these, er, people?

Moses: In the Sinai wilderness.

Ahmed (*to Yousef*): He's not only a smart aleck, he doesn't tell the truth. No one would be stupid enough to herd people in the Sinai wilderness for forty years.

Yousef: Thank you very much. We'll tell you later if you got the job.

(*Moses exits.*)

Ahmed: Next.

(*David enters.*)

Yousef: What's your name?

David: David.

Yousef: Are you an experienced shepherd?

David: Oh, yes, sir. I started taking care of my father's flocks when I was just a boy. I killed a lion and a bear when I was still a teenager.

Yousef: How did you do that?

David: With a sling shot, sir. I can aim rocks very well.

Yousef: What else have you killed?

David: Well, I killed a giant once. His name was Goliath.

Yousef: A giant, huh?

David: Yes, sir.

Yousef: Why do you want to be a shepherd?

David: Because I like to take care of the animals. I even play music for them on my lyre; music helps them relax.

Yousef: I see. You kill lions, bears, and giants, and you serenade sheep.

David: Yes, sir. I am a very good shepherd.

Ahmed (*to Yousef*): This one's a daydreamer. He probably never even *saw* a giant, and he couldn't have killed a lion or a bear. I wouldn't be surprised if he dreams of being a king some day!

Yousef (*to David*): Thank you very much. We'll tell you later if you got the job.

(*David exits.*)

Ahmed: Next. (*Amos enters.*)

Yousef: What's your name?

Amos: Amos.

Yousef: What job are you seeking?

Amos: A shepherd's job, sir.

Yousef: You don't look like a shepherd.

Amos: Well, I am. I have herded sheep many years in Tekoa. That's just six miles from Bethlehem.

Yousef: Yes, I know. What do you like best about being a shepherd?

Amos: I like to watch the sheep. They're fine animals. But even better, being a shepherd gives me time to talk to God. Sometimes when I sit on a hillside under a sycamore tree watching the sheep, God and I talk to each other.

Yousef: God talks to you?

Amos: Oh, yes. Once He told me to tell the people of Israel and Judah to repent from their evil ways.

Yousef: Do you spend a lot of time carrying on conversations with God?

Amos: Yes, but talking to God doesn't keep me from watching the sheep. I'm a good shepherd.

Ahmed (*to Yousef*): He sounds like a wacko.

Amos: God has called me to be a prophet, but I'm still a good shepherd.

Yousef: Thank you very much. We'll tell you later if you got the job.

(*Amos exits.*)

Ahmed: Next.

(*Jesus enters.*)

Yousef: What's your name?

Jesus: Jesus.

Yousef: Why do you want this job?

Jesus: I enjoy taking care of living things. If they get hurt, I fix their wounds, and I carry them if they need help. I like to make sure they're safe. And, I'm the best shepherd you'll ever find.

Yousef: Why do you think you're a better shepherd than anyone else?

Jesus: I'm very experienced, sir. And I'm willing to die for my sheep.

Yousef: You would die for sheep?

Jesus: Oh, yes, sir. I love them very much.

Yousef: But they're only sheep. Surely your life is worth more than that.

Jesus: God loves all His creation.

Yousef: And because God loves them, you are willing to die for them?

Jesus: Yes. In fact, God sent me here to die for His sheep.

Yousef: Why?

Jesus: To be a sacrifice for their sins.

Yousef: You, a sacrifice?

Jesus: Yes.

Yousef: You mean you will become like one of the lambs we sacrifice in the temple as a sin offering?

Jesus: That's exactly right. And because I have never sinned, I will be the perfect sacrifice; no animals will ever again have to be sacrificed.

Yousef: You've never sinned?

Jesus: Correct.

Yousef: And you will be the perfect sacrifice?

Jesus: Right.

Yousef (*to Ahmed*): This guy scares me a little.

Ahmed (*to Yousef*): Me too. I think he has delusions of grandeur.

Yousef: If you are so perfect, why are you content to work as a simple shepherd?

Jesus: It is a noble calling. I love to lead sheep to safe places and rescue them when they get into trouble.

Ahmed (*to Yousef*): This one could be *big* trouble. We don't want anyone dying on the job!

Yousef (*nods to Ahmed before he turns to Jesus*): Thank you very much. We'll tell you later if you got the job.

(*Jesus exits.*)

Ahmed: Next.

Yousef: There are no more, Ahmed, and am I ever glad! I couldn't interview one more shepherd today; they are a nutty bunch, aren't they?

Ahmed: Yeah, they were a little off.

Yousef: Maybe there's more to being a shepherd than we know... or maybe there's something about the job that gets to a guy after a while.

Ahmed: Well, let's call it quits for now. Maybe tomorrow we'll get some good men applying for the job.

Yousef: Yeah, maybe. (*They exit together, shaking their heads.*)

Have Hammer, Will Build

Characters: Raymond
Angie

Angie: Hey! What's all that noise?

Raymond: I'm building a hot-pad holder for Mom's birthday!

Angie: It *sounds* like you are tearing down the house!

Raymond: Well, I'm not. I was just hammering nails into the board for hooks.

Angie: How are you going to hang it up? You know Mom doesn't like nail holes in her walls.

Raymond: I don't know. I guess I'll have to pound nails into the wall anyway.

Angie: You do, and Mom will be mad.

Raymond: Then how can I get it to hang on the wall? I know! Glue!

Angie: Mom will *really* be mad if you put glue on her wall!

Raymond: Good grief, Angie! I thought I had such a neat gift for Mom. You're making it sound like there's no way!

Angie: What you need is a carpenter.

Raymond: They're expensive, and I don't have much money.

Angie: We'll figure something out. I wonder how carpenters in the Bible would have handled the problem?

Raymond: I don't know.

Angie: I'm thinking of a Bible carpenter. See if you can guess who he is.

Raymond: Give me a clue.

Angie: I just did.

Raymond: You did not.

Angie: I did too. I said guess who *he* is.

Raymond: Great clue! That narrows it down to a few thousand people. What's clue number two?

Angie: His great, great, great and a bunch more greats grandfather was the famous King David.

Raymond: Honestly, Angie, when it comes to clue giving, you need a bunch of help.

Angie: Quit complaining. Here's a clue that's so good I can hardly stand it.

Raymond: Let me have it.

Angie: An angel appeared to this carpenter three different times.

Raymond: No kidding! I've never seen an angel; have you?

Angie: No.

Raymond: And this guy saw one three times?

Angie: Yeah.

Raymond: Was he building a temple or something super religious? Is that why the angel appeared to him?

Angie: Nope.

Raymond: Then how come the angel visited him?

Angie: It had special messages about his wife and son.

Raymond: His wife?

Angie: Well, sort of. He was engaged to her when the angel visited the first time.

Raymond: What was the angel's message?

Angie: If I tell you, you'll guess right away.

Raymond: That's fine with me!

Angie: How about if I give you a different clue?

Raymond: Okay. Tell me what his wife's name was.

Angie: That's an even bigger clue.

Raymond: The bigger the better.

Angie: Okay, I'll tell you, but I'm giving it away.

Raymond: Cut the hysterics, and tell me her name.

Angie: It was Mary.

Raymond: Like in "Mary, Mary, quite contrary, how does your garden grow?"

Angie: Same name, different Mary. We're talking about the Bible, not nursery rhymes, remember?

Raymond: What did the angel tell this carpenter ?

Angie: The angel said Mary was pregnant with a baby from God, and that they should give the baby a very special name.

Raymond: Ahhh! The baby's name wouldn't be Jesus, would it?

Angie: Yeah.

Raymond: Then the carpenter had to be Joseph!

Angie: Right. I told you the angel clue would give it away.

Raymond: With your clues and my brains, we're a great team.

Angie: What about *my* brains? They thought up the clues!

Raymond: We're a two-brain-power team. We're hot stuff!

Angie: Joseph had two other visits from an angel.

Do you know what the angel told him each time?

Raymond: Probably something like, "Hi, Joseph, built any chairs or houses lately?"

Angie: Get serious!

Raymond: It seems like the message was something about Egypt.

Angie: Right. First, the angel told Joseph to leave Bethlehem and take Mary and the baby to Egypt because King Herod wanted to kill Jesus.

Raymond: Herod was a nasty guy.

Angie: He sure was. He heard that a special baby was to be born in Bethlehem who would be a king.

Raymond: Since he didn't want any competition, he decided to kill all the babies under two years old in Bethlehem.

Angie: That's why the angel told Joseph to take his family to Egypt.

Raymond: God wanted to be sure nothing happened to Jesus.

Angie: After all, Jesus is the Son of God.

Raymond: Yeah. He's more powerful than any king on earth. If Herod had understood that, maybe he wouldn't have killed all those babies.

Angie: What happened when the angel visited Joseph a third time?

Raymond: I know that. While they were in Egypt, the angel told Joseph it was okay to come back to Israel because Herod was dead.

Angie: When Joseph came back, though, he didn't return to Bethlehem. Why not?

Raymond: Questions, questions, questions. Do you never stop?

Angie: Quit stalling and answer.

Raymond: Okay, you big question mark. Joseph heard that Herod's son was king in Judea, where Bethlehem is. He thought he'd better stay away from there, so he went to Nazareth. That's in Galilee. Anyway,that's where Mary and Joseph lived in the first place.

Angie: Right! I knew you were sharp!

Raymond: Of course I am. And while Jesus was growing up in Nazareth, Joseph taught him all about how to be a carpenter.

Angie: Too bad Joseph isn't around today. He could teach you how to hang that birthday present you made for Mom.

Raymond: Maybe an angel will come to tell me how to do it.

Angie: Sure thing, Raymond.

Raymond: So how do you suggest I put this present on the wall?

Angie: I'm no angel, but . . . .

Raymond: You can say that again!

Angie: What I'm trying to say is, I can give you a good suggestion.

Raymond: What?

Angie: Give Mom the present and let her decide whether or not she wants to hang it on the wall.

Raymond: Thanks, Angie, you really *are* an angel.

Angie: I do have my inspired moments. Let's go find a birthday card to go with that present.

Building Better Business

Ship Builders
Noah
Jared

Tower Builders
Heber
Jonas

Wall Builders
Nehemiah
Eleazor
Miriam
Nathan
Dothan

The Ship Builders

Noah: Watch out, everybody; a long plank is coming through!

Jared: That must be twenty-five feet long! What are you making anyway? A house for giants?

Noah: A house? No. For giants? Yes.

Jared: Huh?! What kind of giants?

Noah: Elephants.

Jared: Elephants!

Noah: And hippopotamuses.

Jared: Hippopotamuses!

Noah: And giraffes.

Jared: Giraffes! I get it; you're building a zoo!

Noah: Nope.

Jared: What, then?

Noah: A ship.

Jared: On dry ground, miles from the sea? Are you crazy?

Noah: If I am, so is God. He told me to build it.

Jared: He's crazy, all right.

Noah: I don't think so. He's always been right before.

Jared: Have you ever built a ship?

Noah: No.

Jared: Then how do you know what to do?

Noah: God gave me a blueprint.

Jared: A blueprint!? Ha, ha! Did it fall out of the sky?

Noah: Watch out; more planks are coming through.

Jared (*ducks*): Who is helping you with this crazy project?

Noah: My wife, my three sons, and their wives. And God.

Jared (*sarcastically*): God, huh? Well I hope so! You certainly need His help!

Noah: You're the one who's going to need it.

Jared: What do you mean?

Noah: There's a reason why God told me to build a ship.

Jared: Well, what's the reason?

Noah: God told me He's going to cover the earth with water one of these days.

Jared (*sarcastically*): Oh sure! God's going to turn this land into a sea, just for your benefit? (*Laughs.*)

Noah: No, He's not turning the land into sea for my benefit, but the ship is for my benefit. And I wouldn't laugh, if I were you.

Jared: Well, you're *not* me, you crazy old coot! Who *are* you, anyway?

Noah: Ask them. (*Points to audience.*) They probably know.

Jared (*to audience*): Who is he?

(*Someone in the audience should prompt children to say "Noah" in case no one knows the answer.*)

Jared: They said your name is Noah.

Noah: That's right.

Jared: Well, good-bye, Noah. Happy sailing! You are the craziest builder I ever met, for sure, but your crazy ideas gave me a good laugh! (*He leaves, laughing.*)

Noah (*sadly*): Sorry to hear that my friend. You won't be laughing for long.

The Tower Builders

Heber: Where is everybody going with all those bricks?

Jonas: To the building site, of course.

Heber: What building site?

Jonas: Haven't you heard about the very tall tower we're building?

Heber: No; I have just come from another country.

Jonas: Oh! Well, welcome to the land of Shinar.

Heber: Thank you. Why are you building such a tall tower?

Jonas: So that it can reach into the sky!

Heber: No kidding!

Jonas (*proudly*): Yep! Just about everyone in the city is helping to build it!

Heber: How come?

Jonas: We want to make a name for ourselves and be considered a strong group of people so we can stay here together and not be scattered all over the country.

Heber: Who's we?

Jonas: Everyone in the whole countryside. We're all helping to build it.

Heber: Everyone?

Jonas: Yeah. See that long line of people? Each of them is carrying bricks for the tower and the city walls.

Heber: You say you're building it tall enough to reach the sky?

Jonas: Yes.

Heber: Does God want you to build such a tall tower?

Jonas: Of course He does. He must get lonely up there, don't you think?

Heber: I don't know. But where I come from, we always ask God first if he wants us to build something, especially if it's as big as you're building.

Jonas: When you ask God, does He answer you?

Heber: Yes. He tells us what He wants us to do.

Jonas: Well, we think we know what God wants us to do. Besides, it's very important for us to make a name for ourselves and to stick together. With all the knowledge and all the power that we have amongst us, we can do just about *anything*! God would like that, wouldn't He?

Heber: I don't know; I'm not God. But I'm pretty sure that He wants us to depend on H*im* for strength and power, not on ourselves.

Jonas: Oh, pooh!

Heber: If I were you, I'd give some serious consideration to what God might do about this tower.

Jonas: What makes you think God *doesn't* want us to build it?

Heber: Well, the way you talk, you people in Shinar must want to rule the world.

Jonas: So? Why is that such a bad idea? With a strong city and such a tall tower, we might be able to do it!

Heber: But I'm not so sure that everyone in the world would like to be ruled by people from Shinar.

Jonas: Well, then, they can come join us, and we will rule the world together! It would be easy, since everyone in the whole world speaks the same language.

Heber: You know what I'd do if I were God?

Jonas: What?

Heber: I'd wave my hand around and say, "Rootle, tootle, hinkum sage, everyone speak a different language."

Jonas: Then we couldn't understand each other.

Heber: That's the idea.

Jonas: Then we couldn't work so well together.

Heber: Now you're getting the picture.

Jonas: But why would God want to do that?

Heber: He wants us to work together for Him, not for our own glory.

Jonas: You're strange. I need to keep working, so I'd better go.

Heber: Okay. But, first, tell me. What's the name of this tower you're building?

Jonas: Ask them. (*Points to audience.*) They know.

Heber (*to audience*): What's the name of the tower?

(*Someone should be in the audience to coach kids to say "The Tower of Babel" in case no one knows.*)

Heber: The Tower of Babel? What a strange name. I wonder if they'll ever get it built?

The Wall Builders

Nehemiah: Okay, everybody, I've set up the plans for our repair work. Are you all ready to hear your assignments?

Eleazor: Yes, tell us.

Miriam: Tell us.

Nehemiah: The Tobias family will work on this section of the wall, and next to them will be the Josiahs.

Miriam: But I wanted to work next to the Yusefs!

Nehemiah: If I put you and Mrs. Yusef together, you'll never get anything done.

Miriam: We will too! We're hard workers.

Nehemiah: Only when you're not talking.

Miriam: We won't talk; we'll work!

Nehemiah: You and Mrs. Yusef talk more than two dozen ladies at the water well.

Miriam: Well, I never! I've got better things to do than listen to insults from you!

Eleazor: You'll work, Miriam. We're here as a family to help with this job, and that's what we'll do. Set a good example for the children and work without grumbling.

Miriam: Okay, okay, Eleazor. But don't let him insult me again.

Nehemiah: Next to the Josiahs will be the Solomons. I'll post the rest of the assignments here by the city gate. Find your spot and start working.

Nathan: Who does he think he is, ordering us around?

Dothan: King Artaxerxes sent him to rebuild these walls. They've been wrecked for years.

Nathan: Well, he could be a little less bossy.

Dothan: If he gets too bad, we'll report him to the Samaritan leader, Sanballat. You know what kind of trouble he can cause!

Nathan: Yes. He'll put that big shot in his place. How does he expect us to rebuilt this wall, anyway? It's a mess. There's hardly a section left standing.

Dothan: I don't know. But he seems to think it can be done.

Nathan: Carpenters and masons could do it, but families? How does he expect women and children to help?

Dothan: I don't know. I guess we'll find out.

Nathan: What is that bossy guy's name, anyway?

Dothan: Ask them. (*Points to audience.*) They probably know.

(*Someone should be in the audience to prompt the children to say "Nehemiah" if no one knows the answer.*)

Nathan: Nehemiah, huh?

Dothan: Yes, Nehemiah. (*Pause.*) You know, I wonder if years from now, anyone will remember the big job we did rebuilding the wall of Jerusalem?

Nathan: Probably not, but let's try, anyway. Nehemiah is doing the best he can. It can't be easy getting men, women, and children to work together.

Dothan: No, I guess not. Well, I'm out of bricks; how about you?

Nathan: Yep. Let's go get some more!

Get Me a Seamstress — Quick!

Characters: **Raymond**
Angie

Raymond: Phooey! My good blue shirt has a tear in the sleeve. I guess I'll have to wear something else to church tomorrow.

Angie: You could borrow my blue blouse.

Raymond: And look like a girl? No thanks.

Angie: You could mend it yourself.

Raymond: I don't know how to sew!

Angie: Maybe Mom will fix it for you.

Raymond: Mrs. Wilson asked her to substitue teach a class tomorrow, so she's too busy getting her Sunday-school lesson ready.

Angie: Oh.

Raymond: Think Dad would mend it for me?

Angie: He's all thumbs when it comes to a needle and thread.

Raymond: I guess I'll just have to find something else to wear. I sure could use a seamstress now!

Angie: That would be nice, wouldn't it?

Raymond: Did you know seamstresses are mentioned in the Bible?

Angie: You can't take your shirt back to Bible times to get it fixed, so that doesn't help you.

Raymond: I'll bet you don't know the name of the best known seamstress in the New Testament.

Angie: I'll bet I do.

Raymond: Then tell me!

Angie: Ah, well, her name was, uh,. . . . That's it! She was "Ye Little Old Seamstress!"

Raymond: Very funny, Angie.

Angie: Her name has slipped my mind. Give me some clues.

Raymond: Okay. She's known by two different names.

Angie: I suppose you want me to tell you both of them.

Raymond: Of course.

Angie: That figures.

Raymond: She was famous for her good deeds, and she gave lots of gifts to the poor.

Angie: You're not making this very easy.

Raymond: She died, but Peter prayed for her, and she came back to life.

Angie: Oh, I remember hearing about that! But I can't think of her name.

Raymond: One of her names reminds me of the old tabby cat we used to have that hopped up on your bed every morning and licked your face.

Angie: Old tabby cat? That's a weird clue.

Raymond: Yeah. Tabby. Say it several times.

Angie: Tabby. Tabby. Tabby. Oh! Tabitha! That was her name! When Peter prayed for her after she died, he said, "Tabitha, arise!"

Raymond: And she did. Now, what was her other name?

Angie: You're not being fair! You're making me guess two names for the same seamstress!

Raymond: That's because I know you're smart. You can do it.

Angie: Let's see. Tabitha's other name. Myrtle? No. Agnes? Gertrude? I give up.

Raymond: Her name reminds me of two words that tell us about what Jesus does for us.

Angie: What?

Raymond: First, he knocks on the *door* of our hearts. Door; that's the first clue.

Angie: What's the other word?

Raymond: Jesus waits to come in until we unlock the door of our hearts with a *key*. That's the other clue. Key.

Angie: Door, key. Door, key. Dorky. That describes you to a tee; Dorky! That's what you are, my dorky brother. Wait! That's it! D*orcas*! Her name was Dorcas!

Raymond: You got it! I knew you were smart.

Angie: It was nothing. All I had to do was put together the dorky clues you gave me.

Raymond: You're the dork, you dorky sister.

Angie: Dorcas was a pretty neat lady, wasn't she?

Raymond: Yes. When she got sick, everyone wanted her to live. That's why they asked Peter to pray for her.

Angie: If she were still alive, I'll bet she'd fix your shirt.

Raymond: I'll bet she would too. But since she's not here, I guess I'll have to wear a different shirt to Sunday school.

Angie: Wear your red shirt with the keys all over it. It reminds me of your dorky clues!

Fair's Fair

Characters: Mary
John

Mary: I'm tired of sitting here. Let's go outside.

John: Mom told us to stay in the house until she gets back from the dentist.

Mary: I know, but we've sat here a whole hour. I want to get up and do something.

John: An hour's not so bad. I know someone in the Bible who sat all day, every day.

Mary: Doing what?

John: Helping to settle people's problems.

Mary: That would be more interesting than sitting doing nothing.

John: We could do something.

Mary: Like what?

John: Maybe we could settle each other's problems.

Mary: You? Settle my problems? That's a laugh. I have a problem. I'm bored. And all you can tell me to do is wait until Mom gets back.

John: I think it's pretty good advice, myself.

Mary: Who was this big problem solver in the Bible you're thinking of?

John: Moses.

Mary: The same Moses who led the Israelites out of Egypt?

John: Yup. He used to sit outside all day, and people would come to him with their problems and ask him for advice from God. He'd pray about it and tell them what to do. If someone did something bad, Moses would decide their punishment.

Mary: You mean if we were Israelites and left our house, I mean, our tent, when Mom told us not to, Moses would be our judge and decide our punishment?

John: That's right. Of course, he'd pray about it first.

Mary: There were a lot of Israelites, weren't there?

John: More than a million.

Mary: Then Moses must have spent all of his time settling problems and handing out punishments.

John: You're right; he did. His father-in-law, Jethro, visited him once and saw how hard Moses worked. He gave Moses some good advice.

Mary: What did Jethro say?

John: Jethro was pretty smart. He was used to being a leader because he was a priest of Midian.

Mary: Where's Midian?

John: It's a place in the wilderness where Moses lived for awhile before he led the Israelites out of Egypt.

Mary: Oh. So what did Jethro have to say?

John: He thought Moses was spending too much time settling everyone's problems. So he told Moses to appoint leaders and train them to do what he was doing. The leaders would bring only the biggest, hardest problems to Moses.

Mary: That sounds sensible.

John: Moses thought so too. He took Jethro's advice.

Mary: If Jethro thought Moses was sitting around solving problems too long, maybe he'd think we were sitting too long too. Do you think he'd tell us we could take a walk in the park?

John: He'd tell us to obey our mother.

Mary: I know a judge who didn't sit around the house waiting for *her* mother.

John: Who?

Mary: Deborah. Remember her?

John: No. Are you sure you're not making her up?

Mary: Of course I'm not making her up! She was one of the judges in the Old Testament.

John: If she didn't stay at home waiting for her mother, what did she do?

Mary: She led an army into battle.

John: She was a warrior?

Mary: No, I told you; she was a judge!

John: Then what was she doing in battle?

Mary: Well, being a judge, she would get messages from God. One day God told her to send for Barak, a captain in Israel's army. When Barak came, she told him God wanted him to take 10,000 soldiers and to go Mount Tabor to fight Sisera.

John: Who was Sisera?

Mary: He was the commander of the army of Jabin, king of Canaan.

John: Oh. Did Barak come when she told him to?

Mary: Yes. But Barak said he wouldn't fight Sisera unless Deborah went with him.

John: Barak, a famous warrior, asked a lady judge to go to battle with him?

Mary: Right.

John: I think you're making this up!

Mary: I am not! It's right there in the book of Judges, chapter four! Look it up!

John: Okay, okay! Then what happened?

Mary: Deborah told Barak that she would go with him, but because he had feared to go alone, or didn't believe that God would give him the victory, or *whatever* his excuse was, the honor of killing Sisera would not be his but would go to another *woman*!

John: Oooh! I bet he was embarrassed! So what happened? Did Barak beat Sisera?

Mary: Yes, But he didn't get to capture him or kill him. A woman named Jael did that.

John: *Now* I remember! Sisera ran away from the battle and asked Jael to hide him in her tent. When he was asleep, she drove a tent peg through his head and killed him!

Mary: Right. But you see, the point is, if Deborah had stayed at home, Barak wouldn't have won his battle. That just goes to show you that staying at home isn't always the best thing to do.

John: But if Jael hadn't stayed at home, Sisera might have gotten away.

Mary: I guess you have a point there.

John: I wonder what it would be like to be a judge like Deborah and to hear from God.

Mary: I don't think very many women in those days rode to battle with men. Do you think her parents or her husband ever got mad at her for doing what God told her to do?

John: Naw, they were probably proud of her.

Mary: Maybe Mom will be proud of us if we go to play in the park.

John: I'm no prophet, but I know that Mom will be *more* proud of us if we do what she told us to do! That means we should stay home 'till Mom gets back!

Mary (*sighs*): I hate it when you're right!

Sample the Fare

Characters: Raymond
Angie

Raymond: Hi, Angie! I made us a *great* fruit drink! Want to taste it?

Angie: What does it taste like?

Raymond: I don't know; I haven't tasted it yet.

Angie: Then how do you know it's great?

Raymond: Because I put a whole bunch of yummy things in it.

Angie: I'm wise to you, Raymond. You want me to taste it to see if it's any good.

Raymond: I offered you the first taste because you're such a great sister.

Angie: I'll politely decline and let you have the honor since *you're* such a great brother.

Raymond: Are you afraid to taste my fruit drink?

Angie: Yes! What you need is a special taster to sample everything you make before anyone else does to make sure it's safe.

Raymond: Do you really think my cooking is that bad?

Angie: Let's just say I'*m* not going to be your special taster.

Raymond: Maybe Dad will taste it.

Angie: Don't count on it. In the Bible, they had special tasters to do what you want Dad and me to do.

Raymond: I wish one were here now.

Angie: They were called cupbearers, because they carried the king's cup. Right now, I'm thinking of a famous one.

Raymond: Give me a clue.

Angie: He was a cupbearer to Artaxerxes I, king of Persia from 464-424 B.C.

Raymond: I'll bet he got fat tasting everything the king ate.

Angie: He just took a tiny taste to make sure it wasn't poisoned.

Raymond: Did the cupbearer ever get poisoned?

Angie: Maybe some did, but not the one I'm thinking of.

Raymond: That sounds like a pretty important job. If the cupbearer couldn't tell whether or not the food or drink was poisoned, the king could die.

Angie: Right. The cupbearer had a lot of clout and was a high official of the court. A person had to be real trustworthy to have his job.

Raymond: Then he must have liked his work pretty well.

Angie: Yeah, but one day he became very sad. He started to fast and pray and confess his sins.

Raymond: How come? Did something terrible happen?

Angie: Some delegates from Jerusalem arrived in Susa, the winter home of the Persian kings, to report on how bad things were in Jerusalem for the Jews there.

Raymond: Why did that make the cupbearer sad?

Angie: Because he was a Jew.

Raymond: The cupbearer for a Persian king?!

Angie: Yes, he was a Jewish captive.

Raymond: So what did he do?

Angie: He moped around for four months, fasting, praying, and confessing his sins. Finally, King Artaxerxes asked him what was wrong.

Raymond: He sounds like a nice king. At least he noticed his cupbearer was sad.

Angie: The cupbearer asked for a leave of absence so he could go to Jerusalem and help his people.

Raymond: I'll bet Artaxerxes said yes.

Angie: He not only said yes, he gave his cupbearer letters guaranteeing him safe passage through enemy territory, and he gave him permission to take timber from the king's own forest!

Raymond: Wow! I think this story is coming back to me now. Tell me what happened next!

Angie: When the cupbearer got to Jerusalem, he checked out the condition of the wall around the city and found it was pretty bad.

Raymond: Without a wall, enemies could walk right into the city.

Angie: Right. Then he organized all the people, and they started rebuilding the wall.

Raymond: I think I remember now who the cupbearer was.

Angie: Who?

Raymond: Nehemiah. He even wrote a book in the Old Testament about his experiences.

Angie: You guessed it.

Raymond: Didn't Nehemiah run into a lot of trouble as he tried to rebuild the wall?

Angie: Yeah. Sanballat, who was the governor of Samaria, and a few other local governors didn't like what he was doing. So they made fun of everyone rebuilding the wall.

Raymond: It's not nice to make fun of people.

Angie: Then they told people they thought

Nehemiah was trying to commit high treason.

Raymond: You mean like betray the Persians?

Angie: Yeah.

Raymond: Well, was he?

Angie: Of course not. He just wanted to rebuild the wall around Jerusalem because he knew the city had to be secure before he could train the Jews to live in the old Jewish ways. He knew if the Jews didn't start practicing their religion again, they'd lose it.

Raymond: You mean they weren't worshiping God or using the temple any more?

Angie: No, they weren't. So when Nehemiah finally got the wall rebuilt, he taught them the laws of Moses. Then he began temple services again and made rules to make sure the services continued. He also restored the national purity.

Raymond: What does that mean?

Angie: See, the Jews had married people of other nations and religions. So Nehemiah made them promise to marry only other Jews.

Raymond: He was pretty strict.

Angie: He had to be in order to handle the Jews in Jerusalem, and all their feisty neighbors.

Raymond: I need someone as strong and brave as Nehemiah to taste my fruit drink.

Angie: What did you put in it?

Raymond: Stuff like orange juice, pineapple juice, prune juice, apple juice, a little cinnamon, nutmeg, and curry powder. That kind of stuff.

Angie: Yuck! It sounds like too much of a good thing.

Raymond: You mean you're still too chicken to taste it?

Angie: I'm too smart to taste it!

Raymond: Come on, Angie. Help me out.

Angie: Well, okay. Give me a tiny bit, and I'll tell you if it's good or not.

Raymond: Here's a spoonful.

Angie (*cough, splutter*): Uh, not bad, Raymond. If I were you, though, I'd cut back on the prune juice and spices, especially the curry powder. Other than that, (*cough, cough*) it's pretty good.

Raymond: Great! Here's a whole glassful.

Angie: No thanks, brother! A cupbearer's job is to *taste* only a little, tiny bit!

Raymond: Oh, all right, but you sure know how to hurt a guy's feelings.

Angie: A cupbearer's job is never appreciated. Come on, let's go mix up some *good* juice!

There's a Crack In Your Crystal Ball

Characters: **Johnny**
Sally

Johnny: Look what I've got.

Sally: What is it?

Johnny: A crystal ball.

Sally: So you're going to be a fortune teller?

Johnny: I'm going to have the fortune teller's booth at the carnival next week. I call myself Sultan Suliman, the Sorcerer.

Sally: You're strange.

Johnny: For only twenty-five cents, I will tell your fortune.

Sally: No, you won't.

Johnny: Okay, for a dime.

Sally: No.

Johnny: A nickel, then?

Sally: No.

Johnny: Then I'll tell your fortune for free. Please? I've got to practice.

Sally: I wouldn't let you if *you* paid *me*.

Johnny: Why not?

Sally: Because of what the Bible says about things like that.

Johnny: Oh? And just what does the Bible say, Miss Know-It-All?

Sally: It says that you're not supposed to go to fortune tellers and sorcerers and people like that, remember? Mom and Dad read about it in our devotions this morning.

Johnny: They did? It does?

Sally: I guess you were too busy making faces at me to hear what Dad said.

Johnny: So, tell me what I missed.

Sally: Remember when King Saul wanted to find out if God would give his army of Israelites victory over the Philistines?

Johnny: Yeah.

Sally: God wouldn't tell him, because Saul had

been disobedient, and God wasn't with him any more. So Saul he went to a medium.

Johnny: A what?

Sally: You know, a channeler.

Johnny: Now I remember. She was called "the witch of En-Dor."

Sally: That's right. Samuel, the prophet, had died. He used to give Saul direction from God when he was alive. So Saul told the witch to bring Samuel up from the dead so he could talk to him.

Johnny: The witch didn't want to because King Saul had thrown all the mediums out of the country, and she didn't know it was Saul sitting in front of her now.

Sally: That's right! And Saul had thrown all the witches out of the country because God had commanded that when He gave His law to Moses—God said that people who practice these things are an abomination to Him! You don't want to be an abomination to God, do you?

Johnny: What does "abomination" mean?

Sally: It means something that is particularly filthy—something that God *hates*!

Johnny: Wow. So what happened to Saul when he used a witch to speak to Samuel?

Sally: Samuel delivered God's message, like he always had, and it was not a message that Saul wanted to hear!

Johnny: What did Samuel say?

Sally: He said he wasn't pleased about being called up from the dead to talk to Saul. He explained that God was not answering Saul anymore because Saul had disobeyed God. And, he said that Saul and his sons would die the next day, and that God would give the kingdom of Israel to David.

Johnny (*awed and subdued*): I'm not going to call anyone from the dead. This is just a crystal ball, Sally, and I'm not a witch.

Sally: But you're pretending to be one.

Johnny: Give me a break! It's just a carnival.

Sally: Don't you see, Johnny, using a crystal ball is like bypassing God. He wants us to pray to Him, not to seek help from witches and fortune tellers.

Johnny: I thought it was just a game.

Sally: I know you did, but it's really very serious stuff. And playing around with it tells people that you think witches and fortune tellers and things like that are okay.

Johnny: Well, I didn't know that there was anything wrong with them.

Sally: The Apostle Paul did.

Johnny: So now you're going to throw more Bible stuff at me.

Sally: It's a pretty good place to get information.

Johnny: Go ahead and tell me. What did Paul think about fortune tellers?

Sally: There was a sorcerer named Elymas on the island of Cyprus.

Johnny: Elymas?

Sally: That's right.

Johnny: Sounds sort of like Ellie Mae.

Sally: He was a man, silly, and he tried to keep the proconsul, Sergius Paulus, from hearing about the gospel of Jesus Christ.

Johnny: What's a proconsul?

Sally: A proconsul was a political leader, kind of like a governor.

Johnny: Oh.

Sally: Sergius Paulus asked Barnabus and Saul to tell him about God, but Elymas tried to keep him from becoming a Christian. When Paul and Barnabas would start explaining the gospel, Elymas would tell Sergius they were wrong.

Johnny: So what did Paul do?

Sally: He looked right at Elymas and called him "a

child of the devil." Paul said that Elymas was full of deceit and trickery, and that God would make him blind for a while.

Johnny: Well, did he go blind?

Sally: He sure did. He had to ask people to lead him by the hand. When Sergius saw that, he believed the gospel.

Johnny: I don't think God would strike me blind for using a crystal ball at a carnival. . . would He?

Sally: I doubt it. But why would you want to mess with stuff that God has called evil?

Johnny: Come on. You're blowing everything out of proportion.

Sally: Oh? Elymas wasn't the only sorcerer mentioned in the Bible.

Johnny: Did God strike the others blind too?

Sally: No, but Jesus also warned us to stay away from people like that. When we rely on people like sorcerers and horoscope writers for help instead of going to God, He doesn't like that. It's like putting other gods before Him. And you *know* what the Ten Commandments say about that!

Johnny: Yeah. The first Commandment says, "Thou shalt have no other gods before me." We memorized it in Sunday school.

Sally: Don't you see, Johnny? When you do things like use crystal balls or go to seances or read your horoscope, you're telling God that His promises to always be with you and never allow you to face more than you can handle, aren't good enough for you—that you want to know *more* than God wants you to know, and you want to know it *now*! That's very offensive to God!

Johnny: So, what do you want me to do?

Sally: Couldn't you turn in your crystal ball for an advice booth or something?

Johnny: An advice booth?!

Sally: Yeah. You could call yourself "Doctor Know-It-All" or something. People could ask your advice on all sorts of things, like how to get along with people, how to handle money, and how to get good grades in school. Stuff like that.

Johnny: What would I tell them?

Sally: You could look up advice the Bible gives on things and have it all ready on carnival night. All you'd have to do is look in your little file under the right subject, and there would be your answer. You could even hand out little pieces of paper with the advice on it. You know, something people could stick on their bathroom mirrors as a reminder.

Johnny: But people wouldn't come to a booth like that.

Sally: Why wouldn't they? People go to fortune tellers for advice. You'd just be giving them advice from the Bible.

Johnny: But if they saw it was from the Bible, some of them might throw it away.

Sally: That's their problem. As long as you do what is right in God's eyes, you don't need to worry about them. All of us will answer to God for our own response to God and His message.

Johnny: Sounds like a lot of work though.

Sally: I'll help you, and we can get Mom and Dad to help too. They have lots of reference books we can use. Then when we have a bunch of material put together, you can use it over and over again at lots of other carnivals.

Johnny: Do you really think it will work?

Sally: Of course. Look how popular advice columns are in the newspaper. People like that kind of thing.

Johnny: Maybe you're right. I sure wouldn't want people to think it's okay to put other gods before God—And I sure don't want to be guilty of that!

Sally: Now you're on the right track! Come on, let's get started.

I Spy

Characters: Aaron
Moses
Joshua
Caleb
Beor

(*Aaron and Moses enter*)

Aaron: The spies are returning! And I can see Joshua way out in front of the others!

Moses: So they are! I can hardly wait to learn what they've discovered about the land of Canaan.

Aaron: I know it's a wonderful place, because God told us it is! And it sure will be good to get out of this desert.

Moses: I told Joshua and the others to spy out the land and the people who live in it. If there are very many people and they are very strong, we may have a struggle on our hands.

Aaron: Here they come now.

(*Joshua, Caleb, and Beor enter.*)

Moses: Joshua! Good to see you! And Caleb, You look tired. Hello, Beor. Where are the others?

Joshua: They're outside resting. They're pretty tired from the trip.

Moses: You've been gone forty days looking at the land; what did you find out? Is the land of Canaan as wonderful as we've hoped?

Caleb: The land is rich with food, and good crops grow there.

Beor: But the people are so big and strong, they are like giants! And they live in cities with fortified walls around them. We wouldn't stand a chance in a fight against them!

Moses: What do you think, Caleb?

Caleb: I think we should go right away and capture the land. With God's help, we can do it!

Moses: What do you think, Joshua?

Joshua: I agree with Caleb. With God's help, we will have victory.

Beor: But Moses, the people are huge! They could beat us without even trying. Then where would we be?

Moses: We would be in God's will. Because He wants us to go to Canaan and take the land.

Joshua: Then let us go.

Beor: You can't do that! What about our women and children? They'll be slaughtered, or at least be taken as captives!

Moses: Beor, you spies were specially picked for this job because of your keen observation, your attention to detail, and your ability to return to me with an accurate report. But sometimes you see only with your eyes, not with God's eyes.

Caleb: God will give us the victory; I know He will!

Moses: After all this time and all the miracles you have seen God perform, Beor, don't you believe that God can work another miracle for us?

Beor: I guess so, but the people seem so big, that's all. I just don't think it would be a good idea to attack them.

Moses: God is angry with you, Beor, for not believing that He can give us victory.

Beor (*whining*): It's not just me. All the other spies, except Caleb and Joshua, agree with me. They think the land of Canaan will be too hard to capture.

Moses: God is angry with all of you who don't believe He would have given us the victory. Because of your lack of faith, we Israelites must wander in the wilderness for forty years. That's what God has told me. Only Caleb and Joshua will get to live in the promised land. The rest of us will die before the Israelites get to go into Canaan forty years from now.

Beor: You gave us a job to do and we did it. We checked out the land, and we reported back to you what we thought. If we have sinned, it was not intentional.

Moses: You saw the land with your own eyes, not God's eyes. That's why God is so angry. He has shown you many wonderful miracles. He parted the Red Sea for you, guided you with a pillar of fire and a pillar of cloud. He has met all your needs, and still you question His ability to protect you.

Beor: If you think we can beat the Canaanites, let's attack them now.

Moses: The time is not right. God has told us to stay in the wilderness forty more years.

Beor: You're getting old, Moses. It's time for stronger leadership. I'm going to tell the people to gather on top of the mountain and swoop down on those Canaanites.

Moses: It will do no good, Beor. You and the other spies who doubted God's ability to overcome the Canaanites will die in a plague, and the others who try to attack the Canaanites before God tells them to will die.

Beor: We will see who's right. I'm going to round everyone up now. (*Beor exits.*)

Aaron: Shall I stop him?

Moses: No. I must pray that God will be merciful to us even though some do not believe in His power and don't do what He tells us to.

Joshua: Don't give up. Caleb and I will continue to be your spies and obey your commands.

Caleb: And God's commands.

Joshua: We brought back some grapes from Canaan. Would you like to taste some?

Moses: Grapes? It's been a long time since I tasted fruit. Yes, please, let me have some.

Caleb: Grapes grow big in Canaan, just like the people do.

Moses: Some day, Joshua and Caleb, some day the Israelites will get there, thanks to good spies like you who know that you must see with both your physical and spiritual eyes.

Open Wide, Say Ahhh

Characters: Raymond
Angie

Angie: My throat hurts.

Raymond: Don't come near me! I don't want to get sick and miss the picnic tomorrow.

Angie: Me neither. I haven't missed a family reunion picnic my whole life.

Raymond: Then you'd better take a hot bath and go to bed.

Angie: I don't feel *that* sick. My throat just tickles a little.

Raymond: A tickly throat today can mean a sickly girl tomorrow.

Angie: Oh, be quiet!

Raymond: What you need is a doctor.

Angie: No! If I go to a doctor, Mom and Dad will make me miss the picnic for sure.

Raymond: Not if the doctor says you're okay.

Angie: He'll probably say I have strep throat or tonsillitis or something worse.

Raymond: If you do have strep throat or tonsillitis, you'd better see a doctor fast.

Angie: I wish I hadn't said anything to you about my throat.

Raymond: Doctors are nice people, Angie. If you're sick, they'll help you get well.

Angie: And make me miss the reunion picnic.

Raymond: Maybe not. (*Pause.*) Did you know there were doctors in the Bible?

Angie: Sure. Somebody had to take care of all those people.

Raymond: Guess which doctor I'm thinking of.

Angie: Okay, but give me good clues.

Raymond: He's mentioned in the New Testament.

Angie: I said *good* clues.

Raymond: He was probably the first university-trained medical missionary.

Angie: They had universities back then?

Raymond: Of course, silly. They weren't uneducated people!

Angie: What else can you tell me about him?

Raymond: Paul mentions him in three books of the Bible.

Angie: What did he say about him?

Raymond: He called him a fellow laborer and a beloved physician.

Angie: Then he must have traveled with Paul on his missionary journeys. Maybe he was Paul's doctor.

Raymond: I don't know if he was Paul's doctor, but you're right, he did travel with him. He did some other things too.

Angie: What?

Raymond: He wrote more than one fourth of the New Testament.

Angie: He did?

Raymond: Yeah.

Angie: When did he have time to do that if he was traveling all over the place with Paul?

Raymond: I don't know, but he interviewed a lot of people who had been with Jesus, and he wrote down what they said.

Angie: Sort of like a reporter?

Raymond: More like a historian, because in the Gospel he wrote, he told about things that happened several years before he wrote them down. In fact, he was the first church historian.

Angie: So, he wrote one of the Gospels?

Raymond: Right.

Angie: That's not over one fourth of the Bible. What else did he write?

Raymond: If I tell you, you'll know.

Angie: A good clue is supposed to do that.

Raymond: Okay. He wrote the Acts of the Apostles.

Angie: You're right. Now I do know.--it was Luke.

Raymond: Yep.

Angie: I wonder where Luke was born?

Raymond: Some people think he was a Greek born in Antioch.

Angie: Why do they think that?

Raymond: For one thing, the books he wrote show a lot of interest in Antioch. For another thing, the books of Luke and Acts were written in very good Greek.

Angie: Luke must have been quite a person. Look at all he did. He was a doctor, a traveler, a missionary, a historian, and a writer. How did he manage to do it all?

Raymond: He had to be pretty smart.

Angie: Right now, I could use a smart doctor, someone who can tell me how to get rid of this sore throat before the picnic tomorrow.

Raymond: I'm smart, and I told you what you should do.

Angie: Hmph! You're not a doctor.

Raymond: But I gave you good advice.

Angie: What?

Raymond: To take a hot bath, go to bed, and see a doctor.

Angie: Yuck!

Raymond: If you won't do that, you could gargle with salt water and suck throat lozenges.

Angie: Maybe I'll do that.

Raymond: I'll get you the salt water.

Angie: Thanks, doc.

Raymond: I don't want you to miss the picnic tomorrow.

Angie: Me neither!

Let the Music Ring

Characters: James
Henry

James: Where did my flute go?

Henry: I don't know.

James: I need it right now for the play.

Henry: What play?

James: The one our Sunday-school class is giving about Bible musicians.

Henry: What do you do? Sit around and play your instruments?

James: A little, but we talk about music and the role it played in the Bible too.

Henry: Sounds boring.

James: I think it's fun. I play the part of Jubal.

Henry: Jubal? Who's he?

James: He was the first musician mentioned in the Bible. He played the harp and the flute.

Henry: Are you going to play the harp too?

James: No. Carey has an autoharp she's bringing from home. It looks kind of like harps from Bible times. She'll dress up like a Bible woman and play it.

Henry: My big brother plays a guitar; could I borrow it and be in your play?

James: Sorry, Henry. You have to be in our Sunday-school class to be part of the play. And anyway, they didn't have guitars in Bible times. They had lutes.

Henry: Lutes?

James: Yeah. They looked a little like banjos.

Henry: Who's playing the lute?

James: Our teacher. He got this old lute from a missionary who brought it back from Africa. It's real neat. Our teacher says David might have played something like that when he was tending his father's sheep.

Henry: David, the famous king of Israel?

James: That's the one.

Henry: I didn't know he was a musician.

James: Oh yeah, he was a great musician! Before he became king, he used to play a harp whenever King Saul got upset. David's music would calm him down.

Henry: Really?

James: It's true. And David wrote lots of psalms in the book of Psalms, and I'm sure you know that the word "psalm" means "song." The book of Psalms also contains directions for how to sing the songs, and mentions all kinds of musical instruments. Have you ever heard of the lyre?

Henry: That would be Bobby Bayfield.

James: What are you talking about?

Henry: You know Bobby. He tells the biggest lies you ever heard.

James: I'm not talking about people who tell lies! I'm talking about an instrument called a lyre.

Henry: Does it play honest music?

James: Cut it out, Henry. Lyres look a little bit like harps. How about cymbals, have you heard of them?

Henry: Sure. A dollar sign means money, a plus sign means add things together and . . . .

James: And "x" marks the spot to put tape over your mouth.

Henry: Right! Those are all symbols.

James: Well, they're not what I'm talking about. I'm talking about a musical instrument. I know you've seen cymbals; they're two brass or bronze plates that musicians hit together to make music.

Henry: Oh, those! My big sister's best friend plays the cymbals in the high-school band. Once when she crashed the cymbals together, they almost squashed her nose!

James: Well, they had cymbals in Bible times, too.

Henry: I wonder if people in the Bible went around with squashed noses?

James: They also had trumpets. Some of them, called "shofars," were made out of rams' horns.

Henry: Rams' horns?

James: You know, big male sheep.

Henry: Oh, them. Sure, I know all about shofars. You hold them in your hand and swing them around like a sword. When they hit each other them make a noise, and that's called music.

James: You big joker! You know that's not how the music is made!

Henry: How is it then?

James: You blow on it. And the air going through the rams' horn makes noise.

Henry: Oh, kind of like a trombone?

James: Kind of. The shofar was used to sound the call to battle, or to gather the people together for an announcement. It was a very important instrument.

Henry: What else did they have?

James: Tambourines.

Henry: What in the world are tambourines?

James: They're like little drums you can hold in your hand, and they have little pieces of brass or copper around the edges that touch each other when you hit or shake the tambourine. They sound like both drums and little cymbals.

Henry: A real noise maker; I think I'd like that.

James: Then you would have liked Miriam.

Henry: Was she pretty?

James: I don't know.

Henry: Well, find out.

James: I can't! She lived thousands of years ago!

Henry: Oh, another Bible character, I suppose.

James: Yes. She was Moses' sister. And she played a timbrel. It's a kind of drum. She played it whenever the Israelites were real happy about something or were praising God.

Henry: She sounds like my kind of girl. I like drums. The louder they sound, the better I like them.

James: Julie Adams will be the drummer in our play.

Henry: That tiny little girl?

James: She may be tiny, but she sure can play the drum.

Henry: When are you going to have your play?

James: Next Sunday night.

Henry: Maybe I'll have to come to church for that. I can't miss Julie on the drums. What are you going to call this play, anyway, "The Sunday School Songsters"?

James: No. The play's called "Music Masters."

Henry: I like my title better, but I'll still come. May I bring my guitar?

James: Yes, if you promise not to play it until after the performance.

Henry: Okay. Maybe we musicians can get together and have a jam session.

James: Sounds good. Don't forget the bread and butter!

Henry: Now who's the joker, you old flute player?

Harvest Time

Characters: **Raymond**
Angie

Angie: I sure am tired of weeding the garden.

Raymond: Don't expect me to help you with it! When Mom and Dad asked what you wanted for a summer project, you said you wanted to plant a garden.

Angie: I did! But I could kick myself for planting such a big one.

Raymond: I'm glad you did. I like to eat the beans, carrots and squash that grow here.

Angie: "He who eats garden produce has to weed the garden," Raymond. That's a wise old Chinese proverb.

Raymond: "If I help you weed the garden, it won't be your project anymore." That's a wise old Raymond proverb.

Angie: Smart aleck! Helping me to weed is a way

to repay me for some of my vegetables.

Raymond: You chose to grow a garden. So you're stuck with the weeding.

Angie: Boy! If you ever need help with *your* project, don't come to me! (*Pause.*) What is your project, anyway?

Raymond: I was going to raise worms and sell them to local sporting goods stores, but they all died.

Angie: That figures. You probably didn't take care of them.

Raymond: What's to take care of? They do everything themselves.

Angie: No wonder they died! It's a good thing you didn't plant a garden; all your vegetables would have died, too!

Raymond: Everyone knows I don't have a green thumb.

Angie: I appreciate farmers more now that I know how hard it is to raise a garden.

Raymond: Farming is not for me. I want an easy job indoors where the weather can't cause trouble, and I don't have to weed anything.

Angie: Farming may be hard, but people have been doing it for thousands of years.

Raymond: Some people never learn to stay away from hard work!

Angie: If people didn't farm, you and I wouldn't have anything to eat!

Raymond (*thoughtfully*): Yeah. I guess it's a good thing some people like to farm.

Angie: There were lots of farmers in the Bible. Can you guess the one I'm thinking of?

Raymond: Sure, if you give me the right clues.

Angie: He lived in Old Testament times.

Raymond: What else?

Angie: He had a short name--only four letters.

Raymond: Adam!

Angie: No. This farmer lived in Bethlehem.

Raymond: You don't say! Give me a another clue, and make it a better one!

Angie: He was related to a man named Elimelech.

Raymond: Hmmmm. That sounds familiar.

Angie: He married Elimelech's daughter-in-law.

Raymond: What was her name?

Angie: Telling you that would be too easy. You'd guess the farmer right away.

Raymond: That's why I want to know her name.

Angie: Later, later. Let's see, what else can I tell you? Oh, yeah. He raised things like barley and wheat, and he was a very nice man.

Raymond: No kidding. You can do better than that.

Angie: Okay, here's a real big clue. The lady he married already had a mother-in-law, one whose name was Naomi.

Raymond: Why not just tell me who he married?

Angie: Oh, all right. But I'm practically telling you now!

Raymond: Go ahead, tell me her name.

Angie: Ruth.

Raymond: Ruth, huh? How did Ruth meet this guy?

Angie: She came back with Naomi from Moab, which was her country, after Naomi's husband and two sons died. Ruth had been married to one of Naomi's sons.

Raymond: I think I know who the farmer is.

Angie: Who?

Raymond: His name is on the tip of my tongue, but I can't say it. Tell me more.

Angie: The Jews have this kinsman-redeemer law

that says the next of kin can buy a dead man's property and marry his widow so the dead man's name and inheritance will be protected.

Raymond: What's an inheritance?

Angie: You know, what relatives leave you when they die, like land and money and stuff.

Raymond: Oh.

Angie: Naomi told Ruth to ask this farmer to marry her since she was related to him through her dead husband.

Raymond: And she did?

Angie: Yeah. And he thought she was a really nice, hard-working woman. Have you figured out his name yet?

Raymond: It's still on the tip of my tongue. Can you give me another clue?

Angie: Ruth and this farmer got married and had a son named Obed.

Raymond: Obed! I'm sure glad Mom and Dad didn't name me Obed!

Angie: It was a very respectable name back then. Obed was the grandfather of David, the most famous king in the Old Testament.

Raymond: Oh! Now I know!

Angie: So tell me the farmer's name.

Raymond: Boaz!

Angie: Right.

Raymond: He was rich. When Ruth first came from Moab, he let her pick up barley and wheat in his field that the reapers missed. He even told the reapers to leave grain behind because he liked her so much.

Angie: Do you think it was love at first sight for them?

Raymond: Probably not. People don't look very good when they're hot and sweaty and covered with dirt like farmers are when they are working hard.

Angie: I'll bet they were interested in each other right away.

Raymond: Girls! All you can think about is lovey dovey stuff.

Angie: No, sir! Right now I'm thinking about my garden. You won't get hot and sweaty if you help me pull weeds for only ten minutes.

Raymond: Hey, I'm no farmer. Your plants would probably die if I just walked by them!

Angie: Baloney. Think what Boaz would have done. He would have helped me weed my garden.

Raymond: No, he wouldn't. He'd have hired someone to do it, because he was rich.

Angie: Either way, I'd get help.

Raymond: Okay, okay. I'll help for a few minutes.

Angie: Great! Come on, let's get to work.

Raymond: How did you talk me into this, anyway?

Angie: I didn't. Boaz did.

Raymond: Boaz, when I get to Heaven, I'll have a bone to pick with you!

Roll That Dough

Characters: Heth
Sered

Heth: Woe is me. I have made Pharaoh very angry, and now I am waiting for the guards to take me to prison!

Sered: What did you do?

Heth: Pharaoh didn't tell me. He just sent me to prison.

Sered: Surely you did something.

Heth: Well, once, Pharaoh gave me some money to buy supplies for the bakery. But instead, I spent it on wine—I mean, medicine—for my sick wife.

Sered: Did Pharaoh find out?

Heth: I don't know.

Sered: Is that all you did?

Heth: Well, once I got drunk and didn't come to work on time. Pharaoh had to send someone to my house to get me out of bed. He was mad that he didn't have fresh bread for his meals that day.

Sered: You got drunk only once?

Heth: Well, maybe two or three times.

Sered: Or four or five times?

Heth: Maybe. I can't remember.

Sered: It sounds to me like you gave Pharaoh *many* reasons to send you to prison! What else might he be upset with you about?

Heth: Once I put too much salt in the bread. I didn't taste it before I served it, and Pharaoh was furious.

Sered: Maybe he thought you were trying to poison him.

Heth: I would never do that! I just got distracted, that's all. Besides, salt won't kill anybody.

Sered: I think Pharaoh has good reasons to be angry with you.

Heth: I'll be sent to prison for sure.

Sered: You'll be lucky if he lets you live.

Heth: Oh, no! What will I do?

Sered: Be brave. You've made a lot of mistakes. Try to live this part of your life well.

Heth: Easy for you to say! I wish someone could tell me what will happen to me.

Sered: I can't look into the future, but I happen to know what's going to happen to you.

Heth: How can you possibly know the future?

Sered: The story of your life is recorded in a book called, "The Bible," and I've read it.

Heth: So tell me what happens to me.

Sered: I don't think I'd better. Maybe someone out there (*points to audience*) will tell you.

Heth: How would they know?

Sered: I think they've read the Bible too. As I said, it tells what happens to Pharaoh's baker.

Heth (*to audience*): Well, do you know what happens to me? No, wait, don't tell me. I can't stand to know.

Sered: How about if they tell me?

Heth: Okay, but have them whisper so I can't hear it.

Sered: Okay. (*To audience*): If anyone knows what happens to Pharaoh's baker, come up here and whisper it in my ear.

(*Sered should ad lib here as people whisper the answer to*

him. He *can say, "No, that's not right" or "Yes, that's right." If no one knows, someone should be planted in the audience to give him the right answer.*)

Sered: I got the answer!

Heth: What is it?

Sered: You're not going to like it!

Heth: I'm not?

Sered: In fact, you're going to hate it.

Heth: I am?

Sered: In fact, maybe I shouldn't tell you at all, it's so awful.

Heth: You shouldn't? I mean, you should. Tell me. I've got to know.

Sered (*to audience*): Shall I tell him?

Heth: Tell me!

Sered: Okay. But don't say I didn't warn you.

Heth: Just tell me, okay?

Sered: Okay. You are going to prison. And after a while, Pharaoh will hang you.

Heth: Prison. Hanging? Oh, no! You shouldn't have told me!

Sered: But you told me to tell you.

Heth: I didn't mean it. Isn't there some way I can get back into Pharaoh's good graces?

Sered: No.

Heth: But I'm the chief baker. I bake excellent bread, wonderful cakes, delicious pastries. They're so tender they melt in your mouth. No one can bake as well as I can.

Sered: Pharaoh's mind is made up.

Heth: How can you be so sure?

Sered: Because that's what the Bible says. Once you get into prison, you're going to meet a guy named Joseph. He prays a lot, and God talks to him. You're going to have a dream, and God will tell Joseph what the dream means.

Heth: What will I dream?

Sered: You'll dream that you have three baskets of white bread your head. In the top basket will be all kinds of baked goods for Pharaoh, but the-birds will be eating them.

Heth: What a strange dream! What does it mean?

Sered: Joseph's going to tell you it means that in three days Pharaoh will hang you and the birds will eat you up.

Heth: Then there's no hope. I'm doomed. Why is Pharaoh being so cruel?

Sered: Maybe to teach the other bakers not to get drunk or steal his money.

Heth: Woe is me!

Sered: Try to get your mind off of it.

Heth: Easy for you to say.

Sered: At least you won't be forgotten.

Heth: How's that?

Sered: You're mentioned in the Bible, and I have a feeling people are going to read that Book for a long time to come.

Heth: You mean I'm in a best-selling book?

Sered: Right.

Heth: By the way, why are *you* sitting here waiting for the guards?

Sered: I'm Pharaoh's butler.

Heth: Oh, yes, I thought you looked familiar. Is Pharaoh mad at you too?

Sered: Yes, but he'll forgive me. I know, because I've read the Bible.

Pay Up, Buddy

Characters: Raymond, Angie

Angie: My piggy bank sounds empty. Will you lend me a dollar, Raymond?

Raymond: You're always broke. What do you want a dollar for this time?

Angie: To buy some new clothes for my doll.

Raymond: You want a dollar for doll clothes?! Forget it!

Angie: Some brother you are! Next time you want to borrow money, don't come to me.

Raymond: I won't. You never have any.

Angie: I'll ask Mom. She'll give me a dollar.

Raymond: I wouldn't ask her now if I were you. She's figuring the family's income tax, and she's been muttering a lot.

Angie: Uh oh, that's a bad sign. We'd better not disturb her until she's in a better mood.

Raymond: I'm glad I don't have to worry about figuring income tax yet.

Angie: Me too. But just about every adult has to do it. Even people in the Bible had to worry about taxes.

Raymond: I guess taxes will be around forever.

Angie: Can you name a tax collector in the Bible?

Raymond: Sure.

Angie: Who?

Raymond: The disciple, Matthew.

Angie: True, but he's not who I'm thinking about.

Raymond: So give me a clue.

Angie: He was short.

Raymond: You call that a clue?

Angie: Yes, because this man became famous partly because he was so short. When Jesus came to Jericho, this man wanted to see him. But there were so many people in the crowd he couldn't see over their heads.

Raymond: Poor guy. He should have used stilts.

Angie: Know who he is yet?

Raymond: Timothy Taxman, the stiltless dwarf.

Angie: Get serious.

Raymond: Then give me a serious clue.

Angie: I've given you several. Here's another serious clue. He was a leader among the tax collectors, and he was very rich.

Raymond: Rich, huh? That figures. He probably overtaxed people.

Angie: Be careful. You're judging him before you know the whole story.

Raymond: So tell me more about him.

Angie: Here's a really big clue.

Raymond: Give it to me.

Angie: He climbed up in a sycamore tree so he could see Jesus.

Raymond: A sycamore tree?

Angie: Yeah.

Raymond: That rings a bell. . . Oh! I remember now. He has a long, funny-sounding name.

Angie: Right. It begins with Z.

Raymond: Z. Let's see. Zeak, Zoo, Zipper, Zero, Zack. That's it! Zacchaeus!

Angie: Right! And when Jesus came to the sycamore tree, you know what he said?

Raymond: He said, "Come down, Zacchaeus, because I'm going to your house today."

Angie: Yeah. And the crowd didn't like it. They thought Jesus should avoid people like tax collectors.

Raymond: But Zacchaeus was a pretty good guy. He told Jesus he'd give half his wealth to the poor, and if he'd cheated anyone, he'd give them back four times what he took.

Angie: So he must have gotten most of his money honestly, because if he had cheated very many people, he'd have run out of money trying to pay back four times what he'd taken, right?

Raymond: Right, especially if he'd already given half of his money away!

Angie: Yup. He was determined to be obedient to God, no matter how much it cost him.

Raymond: Listen, it sounds like Mom's muttering again.

Angie: She must be having more trouble with those income tax forms.

Raymond: I feel sorry for her.

Angie: Maybe she needs a break. I'll take her some lemonade and cookies and remind her of how lucky she is to have me for a deduction. Then I'll ask her for a dollar.

Raymond: You're braver than I am.

Angie: On second thought, maybe I'd better wait. I sure would hate to miss out on that dollar.

Raymond: You can give me those cookies and lemonade.

Angie: In exchange for a dollar?

Raymond: No.

Angie: Then get your own. Mom gets hers whether I get my dollar or not. After all, she's a pretty good mom, and she deserves them.

Raymond: You're right. You go get the lemonade, and I'll carry the cookies. Maybe Mom will feel better if we tell her we love her.

Angie: Great idea!

Learn Your ABC's

Characters: Raymond
Angie

Raymond: I hate homework, I hate math, and I hate Mrs. Pritchard.

Angie: Shame on you, Raymond! You know better than to say you hate someone! Besides, I always thought Mrs. Pritchard was a pretty nice teacher, what's wrong?

Raymond: She assigned us two whole pages of story problems for math homework, and I'm stuck on the first one!

Angie: I'm good at math; maybe I can help.

Raymond: Thanks, but I don't even want to think about it. Maybe a hurricane will hit our house tonight and destroy my math book!

Angie: Dreamer. You'd just have to pay for the book, and you'd still have to do your homework or get a big fat F.

Raymond: Then Mom and Dad would ground me.

Angie: What you need is a really good teacher to help you understand math better.

Raymond: If you're volunteering, forget it. There's a teacher in the Bible I could really use now.

Angie: Who was he?

Raymond: Guess.

Angie: Jesus.

Raymond: Good try. Jesus was the greatest teacher of all, but I'm thinking of someone else.

Angie: Aren't you going to give me any clues?

Raymond: He was a highly respected doctor of the law, and he was a Pharisee—you know—one of the Jewish religious leaders.

Angie: When did he live?

Raymond: He was alive when the disciples were spreading the good news about Jesus.

Angie: What book of the Bible is he mentioned in?

Raymond: Acts.

Angie: What does Acts say about him?

Raymond: In one place, it says he saved Peter and some of the other disciples from being killed.

Angie: How did he manage that?

Raymond: The disciples were in Jerusalem preaching about Jesus, healing the sick, and casting out evil spirits. The high priest and the rest of the Sanhedrin didn't like that.

Angie: The what?

Raymond: The Sanhedrin. It was a group of Jewish religious leaders who formed a council to make decisions about things like Jewish law and religious practices.

Angie: Oh.

Raymond: The high priest ordered the disciples arrested and thrown into jail because of what they were doing.

Angie: Poor disciples. Someone was always throwing them into jail.

Raymond: But they didn't stay there long. An angel came that night, let them out, and told them to continue speaking in the temple about Jesus. So that's where they went first thing the next morning.

Angie: They must have been awfully brave to go back to the place where they were arrested.

Raymond: Right! When the high priest sent messengers to the prison to get the disciples, they were gone.

Angie: Uh oh, I smell trouble.

Raymond: Someone told the council members that the disciples were in the temple preaching. So the high priest sent people to get them and bring them before the council.

Angie: They must have been furious by then.

Raymond: Yep. The high priest was really mad. He said, "We told you guys to stop preaching about Jesus, but you're still doing it, and you're accusing us of putting Jesus to death."

Angie: Well, they *were* responsible for having Him crucified!

Raymond: Peter told the high priest that he and the other disciples thought it was more important to obey God than to obey the council.

Angie: Right on, Peter! Keep preaching.

Raymond: He also said that Jesus, whom they had crucified, was now exalted by God, and was the Savior of Israel and could forgive their sins.

Angie: I'll bet that made them so mad their faces turned purple.

Raymond: It made them so mad they wanted to kill Peter and the other disciples.

Angie: I wonder if the disciples wished Peter had kept his mouth shut.

Raymond: I don't think so. They agreed with what he was saying. If he hadn't said it, they probably would have.

Angie: What happened next?

Raymond: This great teacher I'm thinking about stood up and gave the other council members some good advice. They listened because they respected him so much.

Angie: What did he say?

Raymond: He told them not to harm the disciples. He said that if they were just a bunch of trouble makers, they would soon disappear. But if they were from God, the council could not do anything to stop them. And if they tried, they would be fighting against God.

Angie: Good advice.

Raymond: The high priest and the rest of the council thought so too, but they were still mad. They gave orders for the disciples to be beaten, and told them to quit teaching about Jesus. Then they let them go.

Angie: I'll bet they didn't stop preaching.

Raymond: You've got that right! They praised God for letting them suffer for Him. Then they went back to the temple to tell people about Jesus.

Angie: That's a great story, Raymond, but it hasn't helped me figure out who the teacher is.

Raymond: I can give you one more clue, but it's a real big one.

Angie: Let's have it.

Raymond: Paul said he had been taught Jewish law by this great teacher in Jerusalem before Paul became a Christian.

Angie: Paul was his student, huh?

Raymond: Yeah. Paul was a Pharisee just like his teacher was.

Angie: Let's see. He was a Pharisee. He taught Paul, and he saved Peter and some of the other disciples from dying. Of course! Now I know! He was Gamaliel!

Raymond: Right.

Angie: He was a very wise man.

Raymond: I'll bet he'd know the answer to this math problem right away.

Angie: Too bad he isn't here to help you. But I'm here, and I can help.

Raymond: I don't know who else to ask, so I guess I'm stuck with you.

Angie: Stuck with me! Keep talking, buster, and I won't help you at all.

Raymond: Okay, okay. Forget the stuck part. See if you can figure this out.

Polish That Silver

Characters: **Demetrius**
Jasper
Solon
Gaius
Aristarchus
Jason

Demetrius: Quiet, please, and listen to what I have to say.

Jasper: We're listening, Demetrius.

Demetrius: I have called all of you silversmiths together today in this meeting place because we have a problem.

Jasper: We do?

Solon: Yes, we do. It's that teacher fellow named Paul and the others who travel with him.

Demetrius: You're right. He and his fellow missionaries are telling people there are no gods made with human hands. They claim the Jewish God, Jehovah, is the only God, and that Jesus Christ is His Son.

Jasper: What!?

Solon: To say that is to speak against the great goddess Diana! They must be stopped!

Demetrius: Diana can't be treated that way!

Jasper: Yesterday someone who used to be a good customer refused to buy one of my silver shrines to Diana because he said Jehovah is the only true God. It was a beautiful shrine too; it would have brought lots of money.

Solon: I worked for days over one silver masterpiece. I pounded and shaped the silver into delicate, paper-thin leaves. You know what happened to it?

Jasper: What?

Solon: A child with some of those zealous parents who have been listening to Paul picked it up and threw it on the ground!

Jaspar: No! What an awful thing to happen!

Solon: The silver leaves shattered. My masterpiece was ruined. The parents apologized and paid for the damage, but it should never have happened.

Jasper: What is our city coming to if even children believe these lies that Paul preaches?

Demetrius: Paul isn't stopping here. He's taking his message all over Asia.

Solon: We've got to stop him!

Demetrius: If he continues teaching, we could be out a job. No one will want to buy shrines built for gods and goddesses who they no longer believe in!

Jasper: Making shrines is half my business! I also make necklaces, bracelets and other jewelry. But they don't bring in enough money to feed my family.

Solon: I specialize in making shrines and silver-plated idols. I'm very good at covering the wooden figures of idols with thin sheets of silver and pounding the sheets carefully into place. My wife and children will become beggars if I can't continue my work.

Jasper: Paul and his bunch of teachers are a menace to Ephesus.

Demetrius: He's even telling people not to go to the temple of Diana anymore! He says her images should be destroyed.

Jasper: Where is that awful man? Let me get my hands on him! I'll wring his neck.

Demetrius: I've sent someone to bring him here so we can tell him to stop preaching!

Solon: Good for you.

((*Gaius and Aristarchus enter.*)

Gaius: Someone just dragged us in here!

Aristarchus: What do you want with us?

Demetrius: Do you work with Paul, the preacher?

Gaius: Yes.

Demetrius: Where is Paul?

Aristarchus: He's unavailable right now.

Demetrius: In hiding, I'll bet. What are your names?

Gaius: I'm Gaius.

Aristarchus: I'm Aristarchus.

Demetrius: What do you mean telling people there are no gods made by human hands? Our great goddess Diana is angry with you!

Gaius: Diana is not angry. She can't be angry, she's not real. She's just an image made by silversmiths like you. Jehovah is the only God, and Jesus Christ is His Son.

Solon: Cut out his tongue!

Demetrius: What do you have to say for yourself, Aristarchus?

Aristarchus: If you cut out our tongues, others will take our places to tell the truth about God.

Demetrius: You are thieves, stealing our livelihood. Don't you realize that your teaching is hurting our business?

Solon: People aren't buying as many of our shrines because of your teachings. You must stop telling people that Diana is not a god.

Gaius: You are all fine silversmiths; make something besides shrines for Diana. Make silverware or bowls or other useful things. People will buy them, because you make such beautiful things.

Jasper: Don't tell us how to run our businesses!

Solon: You have a lot of nerve, trying to tell us how

to run our business and what to make!

Aristarchus: We admire your silver work. But we want people to know about the one, true God.

Demetrius: You people are nothing but trouble.

Solon: In the name of the great Tubalcain, the first metal worker ever mentioned, I promise to keep these false teachers from speaking against Diana.

Jasper: Yes, Solon! (*Turns to Gaius and Aristarchus*): You false teachers take this message back to Paul, "Great is the goddess Diana!"

Demetrius, Jasper and Solon (*all together*): Great is the goddess Diana! Great is the goddess Diana! Great is the goddess Diana!

(*Jason enters.*)

Jason: Quiet, all of you. As the town clerk, it's my duty to tell you that you're making too much noise. You could get us all in trouble for creating such a disturbance.

Demetrius: These men are ruining our silversmith trade! And they are telling people that Diana is not a goddess at all!

Jason: People all over the world know that Ephesians worship the goddess Diana. And everyone here knows what good silversmiths you are.

Demetrius: Thank you, Jason. But these teachers say there is no god but Jehovah. They are enemies of Diana.

Jason: Don't let that bother you. The Ephesians already know about Diana. Not even Paul with all his teaching ability can change that.

Solon: But they're hurting our business.

Jason: Have they personally pushed people away from your door? Have they put their hands into your pockets to steal money? Have they destroyed any shrines or idols that you've made?

Demetrius: Well, no, but . . . .

Jason: If they have broken the law, take them to court. But if you don't have anything to charge them with, let them go and quit making such a fuss.

Demetrius: But we have to defend our livelihood.

Jason: Then go home and work. That will defend your livelihood. You can't create things out of silver when you're spending all your time complaining. Now go home, all of you.

Solon: Come on, Jasper, there's no point in sticking around.

Jasper: Okay. But if I ever see Paul and his gang near my silversmith shop, I'll get the whole neighborhood after them. They're troublemakers.

Demetrius: Gaius and Aristarchus, you will leave town if you know what's good for you. And take Paul with you. He's the biggest troublemaker of all.

Gaius: We don't want to cause trouble. We came here to tell you the truth about God and Jesus Christ, so you can know the truth and be set free from idol worship.

Demetrius: See what I mean, Jason? They never stop preaching. They're trying to destroy our business.

Jason: Go back to work, Demetrius. Our goddess Diana is too great to be damaged by the foolish talk of these men that there is only one god.

(*Demetrius, Solon and Jasper exit, complaining under their breaths.*)

Gaius: Thank you, Jason.

Jason: Don't thank me. Just leave. You've caused enough trouble as it is.

Aristarchus: You are a fair and honest man. God bless you.

Gaius: Someday we hope you will discover how wonderful it is to know the one true God.

Jason: Don't start preaching to me! Take my advice and leave before you get into more trouble.

(*Gaius and Aristarchus exit.*)

Jason: Silversmiths are so touchy about their art work. Maybe if I buy some of their silver work for the city of Ephesus, they'll feel less threatened by these religious teachers!

This Is the House That God Built

Characters: **Bezaleel**
Zibiah
Aholiab

Bezaleel: Guess what, Zibiah?

Zibiah: What, my husband?

Bezaleel: Moses has made me the head craftsman of the tabernacle project!

Zibiah: How wonderful!

Bezaleel: I'm to be in charge of building the tent that will be God's house. Can you imagine such an honor?

Zibiah: You deserve it, Bezaleel. You're an expert at working with gold, silver, brass, stone, and wood. And you are good at getting others to work together, too.

Bezaleel: I appreciate your confidence, but this is such a big project, and so important; I wonder if I can do it?

Zibiah: Moses wouldn't have appointed you if he didn't think you could handle the job.

Bezaleel: Moses said if I didn't know how to do something, I should pray about it and God would show me.

Zibiah: That's good advice.

Bezaleel: Moses appointed Aholiab to help me.

Zibiah: Oh, yes, he's from the tribe of Dan. He'll do very well. He's an excellent weaver.

Bezaleel: I can't get over what a big honor this is. Me, the head builder of the tabernacle!

Zibiah: Your grandfather Hur would be so proud of you! He couldn't have known when he was helping Moses hold up his tired arms, that his grandson would build the tabernacle.

Bezaleel: Moses reminded me of that today. He said God's command that he hold up his hands all day long during the battle against the Amalekites seemed too hard. But everytime he lowered his arms to rest, the Israelites began to lose. Just when he thought he couldn't keep his hands up any longer, God sent men like my grandfather Hur to help him. Moses said that if I need help, God will send people to me also.

Zibiah: Moses is a wise man.

Bezaleel: Well, I'd better get busy with my task.

Zibiah: Yes, there is a great deal to do.

Bezaleel: The first thing is to ask the Israelites to

donate some of their gold, silver, fine cloth, and precious stones for the tabernacle. Do you think you could go among the women and ask them to do that?

Zibiah: Of course, I'd be happy to. And I'll donate my own gold necklace.

Bezaleel: But your grandmother gave that necklace to you; it's a family heirloom.

Zibiah: I can't imagine a better place for it than among the gold that will decorate God's house.

Bezaleel: Thank you, Zibiah. God will honor your gift.

(*Zibiah exits.*)

Bezaleel: I'd better get Aholiab. He needs to be in on the planning too. (*Calls offstage:*) Aholiab, will you come in here, please?

Aholiab (*entering*)**:** Here I am.

Bezaleel: We need to make plans for working on the tabernacle.

Aholiab: I'm so excited that Moses chose me to help you. Think what an honor it is to be building the house of God!

Bezaleel: We must begin every workday with prayer.

Aholiab. I agree. That's the most important part of our plans. Then God will give us wisdom and direct our thoughts so we can build this tabernacle the way He wants it built.

Bezaleel: Let's start right now.

Aholiab: Okay. (*They bow their heads.*)

Bezaleel: Dear God, as Aholiab and I talk together about Your plans for the tabernacle, give us the wisdom we need to build it as You want it done. Help our hands to work skillfully and our minds to be clear and sharp so the finished product will honor You.

Aholiab: Amen.

Bezaleel: Now, Aholiab, I want to you to be in charge of engraving, embroidering, and weaving. You have a good eye for design and you will do well in that area.

Aholiab: Thank you, Bezaleel, I'll be glad to accept that responsibility.

Bezaleel: There are curtains to make for the sides of the tabernacle, and we need ram's skin and badger's skin coverings for the roof. We'll also need special garments for the priests.

Aholiab: I can get help; there are lots of talented people among the Israelites.

Bezaleel: I also need you to find someone who can make all the utensils we need. We need dishes, cups, bowls, and pitchers, and we need a very special candlestick. It will take someone who is good at pounding gold into intricate designs. Do you think you can find such a person?

Aholiab: I'll do my best. I see that God has designed something very special for the priests' garments. He wants a breastplate woven of gold, blue, purple and red linen, with twelve precious stones set in it, one for each of the twelve tribes of Israel; won't that be beautiful?

Bezaleel: Yes indeed. And the stones are to be mounted in gold settings with the names of the twelve tribes to be engraved in gold.

Aholiab: Yes, and the priests are to have a special garment, called an ephod, which will be fastened at the shoulders with chains of pure gold.

Bezaleel: If you take care of all that, I can handle the furniture and the wood supports for the tabernacle. Let's see, we'll need an ark, a table, lampstand, altar, and a laver in which the priests can wash their hands and feet.

Bezaleel: Yes. God has given detailed instructions for each part of the priests' clothing and each part of the tabernacle. We must be careful to follow His instructions exactly.

Aholiab: I'll get busy right now, finding some talented artists to help me.

Bezaleel: Good.

(*Aholiab exits, Zibiah enters.*)

Zibiah: You'll never believe it, Bezaleel.

Bezaleel: What will I never believe?

Zibiah: I told several of the women about how God wants gold, silver, fine linen, and jewels for the tabernacle, and they organized themselves into groups and went to every single tent in the whole camp! And you know what?

Bezaleel: What?

Zibiah: *Everybody* donated something! We started bringing it all to Moses, and he finally told us to stop because we have more than we'll ever need!

Bezaleel: That's wonderful, Zibiah! Such generosity shows how much everyone loves the Lord God!

Zibiah: Yes, God inspired them. We can feel God's presence in this project, Bezaleel. Everyone is cooperating and talking and laughing together; it's wonderful!

Bezaleel: I'm glad.

Zibiah: Me too.

Bezaleel: I love working with my hands and seeing beautiful things take shape, but this project is beyond my wildest dreams! Building the tabernacle is so important that when I realize I'm in charge, I tremble.

Zibiah: You'll do fine, and your name will be remembered for this project.

Bezaleel: You think so?

Zibiah: What greater task could there be than building the house of God? Moses will see to it that your name goes down in the history of our nation.

Bezaleel: See what you think of this, Zibiah. I've been making a model for the ark of the covenant according to the plans set forth by God; how does it look?

Zibiah: The ark of the covenant? Oh, that is the container that will hold the two stone tablets on which God wrote the ten commandments, right?

Bezaleel: That's right.

Zibiah: I can see from your model that it will be quite majestic. It *should* be majestic, since it will hold such important items.

Bezaleel: Yes. God's plans call for acacia wood. It will be forty-five inches long, twenty-seven inches wide and twenty-seven inches high.

Zibiah: That's a big chest!

Bezaleel: It will be overlayed with pure gold inside and outside, with a molding of gold all around it.

Zibiah: That will be beautiful!

Bezaleel: On the top, it will have a mercy seat to show that although God expects us to follow His commandments, He is also patient and willing to forgive us.

Zibiah: Very good.

Bezaleel: And on the sides will be two cherubim made of solid gold with their wings spread out over the mercy seat.

Zibiah: Oh! Golden cherubim! How excellent that will be!

Bezaleel: And, in order to move the ark, God has instructed us to put a ring at each corner of the ark and make poles to fit through the rings.

Zibiah: Acacia wood would be strong enough for that.

Bezaleel: That is exactly the wood that God has chosen. And I am to cover the poles with gold.

Zibiah: The people have donated more than enough gold for that.

Bezaleel: Yes, and the plans are well under way. Thanks for your help, Zibiah. I'd better tell Moses about how our preparations are going. He'll want to know. There's so much to do, I hope I get everything straight.

Zibiah: You will. We are blessed, Bezaleel. We are helping to build the house of God. He will give you the ability you need, I know. God is great!

Lock 'Em Up!

Characters: Raymond
Angie

Angie: Aha! You have to go to jail.

Raymond: I hate that "go to jail" card.

Angie: While you're in jail, I'll land on all the property and buy it.

Raymond: I hate playing Monopoly with you. You always win.

Angie: I love this game.

Raymond: What I need is a way to break out of jail fast.

Angie: Just roll doubles, and you'll be out.

Raymond: I mean something spectacular.

Angie: Like an earthquake?

Raymond: Yeah! That reminds me of a character in the Bible. He almost killed himself after an earthquake.

Angie: I suppose you want me to guess who he is.

Raymond: Yes.

Angie: Give me a hint. A good one.

Raymond: I want you to guess what he did for a living.

Angie: No fair!

Raymond: You're a good sport. You'll do it.

Angie: Oh, all right. I'll humor you while you're in jail. How come this guy almost killed himself after the earthquake?

Raymond: Because he thought he'd failed to do his job well.

Angie: What was he, some kind of earthquake control person?

Raymond: No, silly! Nobody can keep an earthquake from happening. Except God.

Angie: Tell me more.

Raymond: He was in charge of a lot of people.

Angie: Like a king?

Raymond: No. The people he was in charge of were in a building when the earthquake happened.

Angie: Did the building fall on them?

Raymond: No, they were all safe, but at first he didn't know that.

Angie: Where was this building, anyway?

Raymond: In Philippi, a major city of Macedonia.

Angie: You'll have to give me more clues if I'm going to guess this one.

Raymond: Paul and Silas were in Philippi preaching when the earthquake hit.

Angie: Is this supposed to be leading up to a clue? Don't take forever.

Raymond: There was a young slave girl in Philippi who had a spirit in her that could tell the future. The people who owned her made money by having it tell people's fortunes. Paul cast out the spirit out of her.

Angie: Her owners probably didn't appreciate that!

Raymond: They were furious. She couldn't tell the future anymore, so she couldn't make money for them. They were so mad they had Paul and Silas arrested and thrown into in jail.

Angie: Then what happened?

Raymond: An earthquake hit at midnight. It

opened all the prison doors and made the prisoners' chains and stocks fall off.

Angie: Did this happen in the building this guy you're thinking about was in charge of?

Raymond: Yes.

Angie: Then he must have been the jailer.

Raymond: Right! He figured the prisoners had escaped, and he'd be in big trouble. So he drew a sword to kill himself. But Paul yelled out for him not to harm himself because all the prisoners were still there.

Angie: Why didn't they run away?

Raymond: I don't know. Anyway, the jailer was so grateful no one escaped that he asked Paul and Silas what he must do to become a Christian.

Angie: What did they say?

Raymond: Paul told him to believe in the Lord, and then he baptized the jailer and all his family!

Angie: What a night that jailer had! He went from almost killing himself to finding eternal life!

Raymond: It was a night he would never forget. Paul and Silas were awake before the earthquake. Do you know why?

Angie: Probably because they couldn't sleep in their jail cell.

Raymond: I'm sure they were uncomfortable—especially since they had been whipped and put in stocks—but that's not why they were awake.

Angie: Maybe they were hatching an escape plot.

Raymond: No. They were praying and praising God.

Angie: In jail? I don't think I'd praise God if I were in jail--especially if I'd just been whipped!

Raymond: But look what happened. The jailer and his whole family became Christians. It sounds to me like the prayers of Paul and Silas paid off big time!

Angie: Yeah, I remember this story now. And after his whole family had been baptized, the jailer took Paul and Silas back to jail so he wouldn't be in trouble with the city leaders. But the next day, the leaders released them.

Raymond: And told them to get out of town. What they didn't know was that Paul and Silas left a whole family of new converts behind.

Angie: I'll bet they never would have arrested Paul and Silas if they had known what effective witnesses they were going to be in jail.

Raymond: I'll bet you're right. And I'll bet if I don't get doubles on this next throw so I can get out of jail free, there's going to be an earthquake. This Monopoly board will jump all over the place.

Angie: No fair cheating. You touch that board, and you'll wish you hadn't.

Raymond: Just kidding.

Angie: If you don't get doubles, maybe I'll visit you in jail as I breeze around the board buying up all the property.

Raymond: You would too.

Angie: Be a good sport. I was a good sport when you made me guess the jailer without a name.

Raymond: That's true. Let's keep playing.

Angie: Without earthquakes. Or even tremors.

Raymond: Okay. Give me those dice so I can roll doubles and get out of this jail!

The Grape Juice Stand

Characters: **Asa**
Ozias

Asa: My father has the best vineyard in the whole valley.

Ozias: No, he doesn't. My father's vineyard is much better.

Asa: It is not.

Ozias: It is too.

Asa: Is not.

Ozias: Everyone knows that a vineyard built on a gently sloping hillside is the best place to grow grapes.

Asa: There's nothing wrong with growing grapes in a flat valley. My father's grapes are sweeter than anyone else's.

Ozias: My father's grapes make the best raisins and wines of anyone's.

Asa: I must admit, your raisins are pretty good. My father doesn't make them. He says they're too much trouble.

Ozias: You know why my father's raisins are the best?

Asa: Why?

Ozias: Because in October when the grapes are at their ripest, father spreads them in bunches on the ground and pours olive oil over them.

Asa: Why olive oil?

Ozias: To keep them moist.

Asa: Oh.

Ozias: He turns the grapes over a lot too.

Asa: No wonder my father doesn't make raisins. They sound like an awful lot of work.

Ozias: When they're dry enough and all shriveled up, Father stores them in jars.

Asa: And sells them for twice what they're worth in the market!

Ozias: He sells them at a fair price! My father doesn't cheat.

Asa: Okay, okay. I guess he has to charge more because of all the work it takes to dry them.

Ozias: What about your father? He charges an awful lot for the honey he makes from his grapes.

Asa: No, he doesn't.

Ozias: He does too.

Asa: He does not. Honey isn't easy to make.

Ozias: I thought your father didn't like hard work.

Asa: My father isn't lazy! You apologize for saying that!

Ozias: All right, your father isn't lazy. But you said he thought making raisins was too much work.

Asa: They're too much work only because he's so busy taking care of the vineyard and making honey from his grapes.

Ozias: Your father does make pretty good honey.

Asa: Yeah, and I help him.

Ozias: I help my father make raisins too.

Asa: You know what I do?

Ozias: What?

Asa: I stir the grapes while they boil in a big pot over a fire.

Ozias: It must be hot work.

Asa: It is. But my father gives me a jar of honey for my very own for helping him.

Ozias: We sometimes eat your father's honey at breakfast. It looks kind of like jelly, doesn't it?

Asa: Yes, and it sure tastes good.

Ozias: I know how to make grape juice from grapes. Do you?

Asa: Of course. I help my dad do that too.

Ozias: You know what we ought to do?

Asa: What?

Ozias: We should start a business of our own.

Asa: What kind of business?

Ozias: We could sell grape juice.

Asa: You mean set up a stand along the road and sell juice to people who walk by?

Ozias: You've got the idea.

Asa: Hey, I like that. Maybe father would let me have some juice to sell.

Ozias: I know my father would give me some juice. I've been real good this summer about watching the weather and telling him when the next day will be sunny and when heavy dew will come at night.

Asa: You can predict what the weather will be?

Ozias: Not really. But father says sunny days and dewy nights are best for grapes, so I predict those most.

Asa: You trickster!

Ozias: I'm right more than half the time.

Asa: Big deal. It's sunny most days anyway.

Ozias: If we're going to have good, sweet grape juice to drink, we need to be sure the grapes run along the ground and are covered with leaves so they don't ripen too fast.

Asa: That's part of my job in my father's vineyard, anyway.

Ozias: Mine too.

Asa: And we have to keep the vines trimmed back.

Ozias: Boy, working in a vineyard is hard, isn't it?

Asa: My father says grapes take more work than almost any other crop.

Ozias: Then why do our fathers grow them?

Asa: Maybe because grapes taste so good.

Ozias: And because the raisins and honey sell so well at the market.

Asa: Maybe. Does your father leave some grapes in the corners of his field for poor people to pick?

Ozias: Yes, of course, he has to; it's the law.

Asa: I've seen some of those poor people go through our fields. They look so hungry, and when they eat the grapes, their faces light up. They just keep eating and eating.

Ozias: You know why they do that?

Asa: Because the law says they can eat all they want, but they can't take any out of the field.

Ozias: That's a good law; without it, our fathers wouldn't have any grapes left in their vineyards!

Asa: Yes, and it's a good law for poor people, too. I'd hate to have no place to get food.

Ozias: Yeah. That would be hard.

Asa: Well, what about our grape juice stand? Are we going to build one?

Ozias: Yep! Let's get to it!

Bait That Line

Characters: **Raymond**
Angie

Raymond: Who moved my fishing box?

Angie: You mean that ugly, metal box that rattles a lot?

Raymond: It isn't ugly. Did you move it?

Angie: No, but I saw Dad put it in the car.

Raymond: Good, then everything's okay.

Angie: Are you two going fishing again?

Raymond: Yeah, want to come?

Angie: I don't know. Are you using worms for bait?

Raymond: Worms, cheese and salmon eggs.

Angie: I'll go if I can use cheese and salmon eggs.

Raymond: What's the matter? Don't you like those cute little worms?

Angie: They jump all around when I try to put them on the hook. I feel sorry for them.

Raymond: Are you a worm lover?

Angie: Well, I don't like to see them hurt.

Raymond: You should learn to fish with nets like the fishermen in the Bible did. Then you wouldn't have to worry about worms.

Angie: Hey, I like that idea.

Raymond: I'll bet you can't guess the name of the fisherman in the Bible I'm thinking of.

Angie: I'll bet I can.

Raymond: Who is he?

Angie: Raymond! Do you expect me to name him without even one clue?

Raymond: Here's your clue. He was married.

Angie: Big deal.

Raymond: Jesus healed his mother-in-law.

Angie: Was he one of Jesus' disciples?

Raymond: Yeah, and that's a big, big clue.

Angie: I'll bet he was James.

Raymond: Nope.

Angie: Then John. You know, James and John, the sons of Zebedee.

Raymond: Zebedee do dah! You're wrong again.

Angie: Are you going to stand there with that silly grin on your face or give me another clue?

Raymond: His brother used to be a disciple of John the Baptist, but when the brother learned about Jesus, he shared the good news with the fisherman I'm thinking about.

Angie: What was his brother's name?

Raymond: You really want me to make this easy, don't you?

Angie: You just want to make it hard for me.

Raymond: All right, his brother's name was Andrew.

Angie: Andrew, Andrew. Hmmmm. And you thought that was such a great clue!

Raymond: It is! I can't believe you don't know who I'm talking about!

Angie: Well, I don't!

Raymond: You wouldn't know a clue if it bit you.

Angie: Oh, be quiet. Did this fisherman do anything famous?

Raymond: Yes.

Angie: What?

Raymond: He walked on water, he caught a net full of fish from a seemingly empty sea, he cut off the ear of the high priest's servant. . . .

Angie: Oh, oh, oh! You're talking about Peter! Why didn't you give me some of those good clues a long time ago?

Raymond: Because I was supposed to be giving *hints*, not telling you the answer! But Peter had another name before Jesus called him Peter. What was it?

Angie: I know that. It was Simon.

Raymond: Good. Now see if you can get this one.

Angie: Another question? No fair.

Raymond: What's another name for Peter?

Angie: Piper.

Raymond: Piper!?

Angie: You know. Peter Piper picked a peck of pickled peppers.

Raymond: Angie! That's not in the Bible.

Angie: I was just checking to see if you were on your toes.

Raymond: I'm on my toes, all right, and if you don't shape up, I'll stand you on your head.

Angie: You try it, and I'll show you my karate chops.

Raymond: Just answer the question.

Angie: What question?

Raymond: What's another name for Peter?

Angie: It just so happens I know that.

Raymond: Then tell me.

Angie: Cephas. That's an Aramaic word. Know how I know?

Raymond: How?

Angie: I read it in our Sunday-school magazine.

Raymond: I'll bet you don't know what it means.

Angie: I'll bet I do.

Raymond: How much do you want to bet?

Angie: If I'm right, you have to bait my hooks with worms.

Raymond: You've got a deal. And if you don't know the answer, you bait your own hooks.

Angie: No problem. Ready for my great answer?

Raymond: I can hardly wait.

Angie: Cephas means rock.

Raymond: Ah, shucks. How did you get so smart?

Angie: Some of us have it, and some of us don't.

Raymond: Brother!

Angie: Even though Cephas means "rock," Peter did some things that weren't very rock-like.

Raymond: Yes, he did get scared after Jesus was arrested and three times denied that he knew Him. But Jesus forgave Peter for being weak, and after Jesus returned to Heaven, Peter never again lost his faith. He became one of the greatest preachers ever to have lived.

Angie: Yes, that's true. It was because Peter became such a great "fisher of men" that the Emperor Nero had him put to death.

Raymond (*sadly*): Yes, Peter died for his faith. (*Brightening up*): But speaking of fishing, are you coming with Dad and me for sure?

Angie: Yeah, now that you're going to bait my hooks if we use worms.

Raymond: Great! Then let's go get our fishing poles!

Make Room for More

Characters: **Raymond**
Angie

Raymond: Hey Angie! Guess what? The Coopers are coming to our house!

Angie: Oh good! When?

Raymond: They're on their way over right now.

Angie: But they can't! My room's a mess, and so is the kitchen!

Raymond: It was your turn to wash the dishes. Why didn't you?

Angie: I was going to do them when I finished my homework.

Raymond: Putting things off until the last moment can get you in trouble.

Angie: Oh, be quiet, Know-It-All. Why are the Coopers coming on such short notice, anyway?

Raymond: They're on vacation. The motel where they had a reservation gave their room to someone else by mistake.

Angie: Why don't they just get another room?

Raymond: There aren't any. There are several conventions in town this weekend, so all the rooms are full.

Angie: I wish I had known they were coming a little sooner. Then I could have been more prepared.

Raymond: The Coopers won't notice. Besides, think how much fun it will be to play with Kyle and Linda. We haven't seen them for two years.

Angie: It *will* be fun to play with kids our own age. How long will they stay?

Raymond: They'll leave tomorrow morning.

Angie: I guess it's a good thing they know us or they wouldn't have any place to stay. Know what? That reminds me of a character in the Bible.

Raymond: What kind of character?

Angie: Sort of an invisible one.

Raymond: You mean a ghost?

Angie: No. But he wasn't actually mentioned in the Bible.

Raymond: Then how do you know he was a Bible character?

Angie: Because something that he *did* is mentioned.

Raymond: You're sounding awfully mysterious.

Angie: He lived during New Testament times, and he was a businessman.

Raymond: If he's not mentioned in the Bible but he was a businessman and lived during New Testament times, what's left for me to guess?

Angie: His occupation.

Raymond: You told me he was a businessman.

Angie: What kind of businessman?

Raymond: I don't know. Give me a clue.

Angie: He lived while Augustus was Caesar in Rome, while Herod was king in Palestine and while Cyrenius was governor of Syria.

Raymond: Did he supply some service to the royal families?

Angie: Nope.

Raymond: Then why did you tell me all that stuff about the rulers? Really, Angie, sometimes you're just plain weird.

Angie: All those rulers are important, because they all had a part in the event that I'm talking about. Caesar Augustus passed a law that said everyone in the Roman world had to be taxed. I thought the other two names might jog your memory a little.

Raymond: They didn't jog it enough. Don't give me any more rulers' names. I hate that stuff.

Angie: Then maybe this will help. Caesar told people they had to go to their *original* hometowns to be taxed—the towns where their ancestors were born.

Raymond: So?

Angie: So people traveled from their homes to other places, because they didn't all still live in their hometowns.

Raymond: I'll bet a lot of people had to travel for that tax!

Angie: Yeah. This one couple traveled from Nazareth in Galilee to Bethlehem in Judea for the tax.

Raymond: Bethlehem, huh?

Angie: Yes, and the lady was pregnant.

Raymond: What does that have to do with the business I'm supposed to guess? Oh, I get it! She went to a doctor to have the baby. You're thinking of a doctor, aren't you?

Angie: No.

Raymond: What, then?

Angie: When people travel, they usually need something once they get where they're going.

Raymond: A pan to soak their aching feet in.

Angie: Maybe, but that's not what I'm thinking of.

Raymond: Let's see. They need a good night's sleep.

Angie: Right! And where do they get it?

nd: At a motel—or at a friend's house if

s.

hey used to call a

me this guy was an

uple traveling to

ey were Mary and

to Bethlehem, they

n, but they couldn't

Raymond: It couldn't have been a botched up reservation, because they didn't have phones or telegrams then.

Angie: How do you think the innkeeper felt when he had to turn Mary and Joseph away, especially when he found out she was pregnant?

Raymond: He probably felt real bad. That must be why he let them stay in the stable with the animals.

Angie: And that's why Jesus' first bed was a manger.

Raymond: I don't think I'd like to sleep in a bunch of straw in an animal-feeding box.

Angie: Me neither. But it must have been better than having no place at all.

Raymond: I guess we're sort of innkeepers for the Coopers tonight, aren't we?

Angie: Yeah. The only difference is the innkeeper in the Bible probably didn't know Mary and Joseph. And he sure didn't know Mary was going to have a baby who would be the Savior of the world.

Raymond: If he had known, he probably would have stayed in the stable himself and let them have his room.

Angie: Wouldn't it be funny if Kyle or Linda grew up to be famous? Then we could put a sign outside our house that said, "Kyle and Linda slept here."

Raymond: I wonder if the innkeeper ever bragged about providing a place for the Savior of the world to stay.

Angie: Probably not. If he had realized who Jesus Christ was, and that He was the baby who had been born in his stable, he probably would have been too embarrassed about making Him be born in a barn to brag about it.

Raymond: What does the Bible say about him, anyway?

Angie: It just says Mary and Joseph laid Jesus in a manger because there was no room for them in the inn.

Raymond: We'll do better than a barn for the Coopers.

Angie: Yeah. Linda can sleep with me in my double bed.

Raymond: And Kyle and I will sleep in the back yard in our sleeping bags—if Mom and Dad will let us.

Angie: Neat! Then their parents can have your room.

Raymond: Now, aren't you glad they're coming?

Angie: Yes. We'll be real good innkeepers and make them feel very welcome.

Raymond: Come on, I'll help you with the dishes before they get here.

Angie: Thanks!

How Good Is Your Shorthand?

Characters: **Elnathan, a reporter**
Baruch, a secretary

Elnathan: Are you Baruch?

Baruch: Yes. And you must be Elnathan from the *Jerusalem Journal*.

Elnathan: That's right. My editor wants me to do a story on everyday life in the city. We carry a lot of stories about the Babylonian seige of Jerusalem, but people are getting tired of reading about food shortages and wounded soldiers.

Baruch: How can I help you?

Elnathan: You've been Jeremiah's secretary for years. I thought our readers might be interested in knowing what it's like to be the secretary of the man who prophecies that the kings of Judah should surrender to the Babylonians.

Baruch: There's never a dull moment!

Elnathan: I suppose you know that people in the street call Jeremiah, "the prophet of doom and gloom"?

Baruch: Yes. Sometimes people even yell "doom and gloom" at us when we walk down the street.

Elnathan: Jeremiah keeps insisting that God has sent Babylon to punish us for not obeying God's laws.

Baruch: That's right.

Elnathan: Babylonian soldiers are breathing down our necks right now; it looks like Jeremiah's prophecies may come true.

Baruch: They *will* come true! Jeremiah really does hear from God.

Elnathan: But a lot of prophets tell the king that *Babylon* will be defeated.

Baruch: Anyone who says that is a false prophet.

Elnathan: Hrrumph! You're pretty sure of yourself, aren't you?

Baruch: No. But I am sure of God, and of Jeremiah.

Elnathan: Well, be that as it may, what is it like to be Jeremiah's secretary when no one wants to hear his message?

Baruch: It isn't easy.

Elnathan: How do you handle the stress of your job?

Baruch: Well, I guess I worry more about the stress that Jeremiah is under than my own. I believe in

Jeremiah's calling. I see the hours he spends in prayer and the way he agonizes over the messages God gives him. I just try to help him do his job the best way I can.

Elnathan: And how do you do that?

Baruch: Mostly, I take dictation. Sometimes I deliver the messages he gets from God.

Elnathan: You mean you write them down on a scroll and then take the scroll to someone?

Baruch: Yes. Sometimes I even read what is written in the scroll.

Elnathan: So you have to deliver the bad news yourself.

Baruch: Sometimes.

Elnathan: Can you give me an example of one of those times?

Baruch: I'll never forget the time God told Jeremiah to write down all the prophecies he had ever been given during his twenty-three years as a prophet.

Elnathan: When did that happen?

Baruch: During King Jehoiakim's reign.

Elnathan: That's going back a few years!

Baruch: I still remember it like it happened yesterday. I spent *months* writing down all the prophecies as Jeremiah dictated. God talks to him a lot, so there was a lot to record. Sometimes I wish God would talk to someone else and give Jeremiah and me a rest.

Elnathan: You must have covered a big time span if there were so many prophecies.

Baruch: Yes. We went back all the way to the beginning of King Josiah's reign.

Elnathan: Oh, yes; Jehoiakim's father. I didn't know him, but I heard he was an evil king.

Baruch: He was! God had plenty to say about what would happen to Judah if Josiah didn't start worshiping God!

Elnathan: Are you saying that if the kings of Judah had obeyed God, Jeremiah wouldn't have had so much doom and gloom to prophecy?

Baruch: I can't say for sure what God would do, but I have a feeling you're right.

Elnathan: I see.

Baruch: I sure wish the people had been more obedient, because by the time Jeremiah finished dictating all those prophecies to me, I had a *bad* case of writers cramp! I couldn't straighten out my fingers for several hours!

Elnathan: Being a secretary has its hazards.

Baruch: Yes. When we finally finished recording all the prophecies, Jeremiah told me to take the scroll to the temple and read it there. He wasn't allowed to go to temple.

Elnathan: How come?

Baruch: I don't know; he didn't explain. Anyway, I did what he told me to do.

Elnathan: What happened then?

Baruch: When the princes heard what was in the scrolls, they were pretty upset. They figured the king would want to kill Jeremiah--and maybe me! They told me to get Jeremiah and hide where no one could find us.

Elnathan: You mean people who get mad at Jeremiah get mad at his secretary too?

Baruch: Oh, yes. They accuse me of influencing him and telling him what to say. They don't realize that Jeremiah really does hear from God. And I *certainly* don't have any influence over God!

Elnathan: So you went into hiding with Jeremiah?

Baruch: Yes.

Elnathan: And what happened to the scroll?

Baruch: When King Jehoiakim heard what was in it, he got so mad that he cut it up, threw it in the fireplace and burned it.

Elnathan: All your hard work went up in smoke?

Baruch: That's right.

Elnathan: How did Jeremiah react to that?

Baruch: He prayed about it, and God told him to write the message over again.

Elnathan: *Again*?

Baruch: Again. So, I got another case of writers' cramp.

Elnathan: It must have taken you *months* to rewrite it!

Baruch: Actually, the second time took only weeks. After all, we were in hiding and had nothing else to do, so we could concentrate on the work.

Elnathan: That's worse than having to write, "I will not pull Sally's hair," one thousand times!

Baruch: Something like that.

Elnathan: So, as Jeremiah's secretary, you take dictation a lot, you sometimes read Jeremiah's prophecies, and you spend a lot of time in hiding.

Baruch: That's right.

Elnathan: Do you worry much about him?

Baruch: All the time. He was thrown into an underground holding tank once when a king became angry with one of his prophecies. Another time, he ended up in a dungeon, and a few times, he has been a prisoner in the courtyard of the guards.

Elnathan: Sounds pretty scary to me! Have you ever thought of looking for another job?

Baruch: Every once in a while. But where else would I find as much excitement?

Elnathan: With your skills, you could work for almost anyone.

Baruch: I suppose so. But Jeremiah told me once that I was not to seek great things.

Elnathan: That sounds like an excuse not to give you a raise!

Baruch: I don't think so. Jeremiah said God would reward me by giving me my life as a prize wherever I went.

Elnathan: Give you your life as a prize? Come on, now.

Baruch: Actually, I took a lot of comfort in that message.

Elnathan: But it doesn't mean anything.

Baruch: Yes, it does. During this turmoil our country is having, God said I would not die. That's comforting to know.

Elnathan: Well, I suppose that is something.

Baruch: None of this would make much sense to someone who didn't love God and feel a strong commitment to His work.

Elnathan: I can see that. My readers may have a hard time grasping why you continue working for Jeremiah when you could be working in a king's palace, surrounded by luxury.

Baruch: But the kings we have don't hear from God, do they?

Elnathan: No, I suppose not.

Baruch: I can't describe to you how exciting it is to write down the words Jeremiah receives from God! It's a little like hearing from God myself!

Elnathan: You secretaries always were kind of religious.

Baruch: That's because we've often been associated with priests. But most of my work is the same as any business secretary; taking dictation and drawing up legal documents.

Elnathan: What's the most interesting legal document you ever drew up for Jeremiah?

Baruch: That's easy. Not too long ago; during the tenth year of Zedekiah's reign, Zedekiah got mad at Jeremiah for prophecying that the king of Babylon would defeat him. So he threw Jeremiah in prison.

Elnathan: Prison must have seemed like Jeremiah's second home.

Baruch: Sometimes. Anyway, while he was in prison, God gave Jeremiah a message.

Elnathan: He did?

Baruch: Yes. He said Jeremiah's cousin Hanameel would visit him in prison and offer to sell him a field, because by law, Jeremiah had the right to buy it.

Elnathan: Jeremiah would be crazy to accept. If Babylon is about to overthrow the whole country, what good will it do to own land?

Baruch: God told Jeremiah to buy the land anyway.

Elnathan: That's crazy!

Baruch: Not really. You have to understand how God works. Sometimes he has Jeremiah act out things.

Elnathan: What would he be acting out by buying land the Babylonians will take from him?

Baruch: It is God's way of telling us that after a time of captivity we will return to Jerusalem and once more own fields, vineyards, and houses here.

Elnathan: So did Jeremiah buy the land?

Baruch: Yes. Everything happened just as God said it would. Hanameel came, and Jeremiah had me draw up a deed for the land. Then he signed it, paid for the land, and told me to put the deed in a clay jar so it would last for many years.

Elnathan: Didn't you ever ask yourself if Jeremiah might be a little touched in the head? I mean, buying land that he couldn't use seems kind of crazy. Surely he won't live long enough to see Judah free again?

Baruch: Jeremiah isn't crazy. I guess you have to be near him to sense the power of God that surrounds this man. But whether or not he lives long enough to enjoy the land is not the point. I explained to you that having Jeremiah buy the land is God's way of telling us that we will one day return to Judah! It's obvious, to me at least, that Jeremiah is a true prophet of God!

Elnathan: And you're his loyal secretary who would say anything to make him look good.

Baruch: My job is to take his dictation, not to be his publicity agent.

Elnathan: I see.

Baruch: You know, Jeremiah has given a lot of positive messages, but people don't listen. He keeps saying that if the people will obey God and surrender to Babylon, God will save the city of Jerusalem from being burned.

Elnathan: Uh, my editor wants me to steer away from political statements. Can we just stick to what it's like to be Jeremiah's secretary?

Baruch: Sorry. It's just that I really believe Jeremiah is giving us God's message, but no one will listen.

Elnathan: What's a normal day like as Jeremiah's secretary?

Baruch: With him, there's no such thing as normal. One minute I can be taking dictation, the next minute we can be hiding from an angry king.

Elnathan: What got you interested in being a secretary?

Baruch: I've always been interested in the law and in recording important events in history. Working for Jeremiah combines those interests.

Elnathan: There's a certain prestige to being a secretary. Didn't that draw you to the job a little?

Baruch: A little, maybe. Many secretaries have an office in the king's palace and play an important role in affairs of the country. Secretaries sometimes keep track of the number of soldiers in the military, and we often keep financial records and give advice to rulers.

Elnathan: Is Jeremiah a pretty good boss?

Baruch: I could use a few more days of vacation, and I wish Jeremiah didn't talk so fast when he dictates, but overall, I enjoy my job very much. As I said, it's like hearing from God myself.

Elnathan: What does the future look like for you?

Baruch: I'll keep on being Jeremiah's secretary as long as he needs me.

Elnathan: What advice would you give young people who are thinking of becoming secretaries?

Baruch: I'd tell them to study hard in school, to learn to spell and do math well, and to have good handwriting. You must also be able to write fast but clearly enough so that people can read what you write. Secretaries also need to know a lot about the law and religious beliefs. They will be called on to interpret the law for people and if they don't know what the law says, they won't be able to do their jobs.

Elnathan: Wow! It sounds like you have to be smart to be a secretary!

Baruch: It helps to be able to remember what you learn. But most of all, the job requires common sense. And you have to be willing to take orders from someone else.

Elnathan: When will Jeremiah get his next big revelation from God? I'd like to get the story for my newapaper.

Baruch: We never know. God speaks when He's ready to. That means we're on call twenty-four hours a day.

Elnathan: Then I'll keep in touch. Thanks for giving me this interview; it has been most interesting!

Baruch: You're welcome. I'll look forward to reading your story. Bye!

Elnathan: Bye!

March In Step

Characters: **Cornelius, a Roman soldier**
Hector, a Roman citizen

Cornelius: Ow! My head hurts. Where am I?

Hector: In a house near Caesarea.

Cornelius: Caesarea? I don't know the name.

Hector: But you must. Before the battle, you said you and the one hundred soldiers you lead were stationed in Caesarea.

Cornelius: What battle?

Hector: The one between you and the mob of Zealots.

Cornelius: Zealots?

Hector: Yes, the ones who want to drive the Romans out of Judea.

Cornelius: I'm confused. None of that means anything to me.

Hector: I know what must have happened.

Cornelius: What? Please tell me.

Hector: You received a very bad blow to your head, and you have lost your memory.

Cornelius: I have?

Hector: I'm afraid so.

Cornelius: But I must remember something.

Hector: Let's find out what you know. What's your name?

Cornelius: It's, uh, it's. . . I don't remember.

Hector: Think hard.

Cornelius: I am thinking hard, but I just can't remember.

Hector: At least we know one thing about you.

Cornelius: What's that?

Hector: You're a soldier.

Cornelius: I am?

Hector: Yes. You're some kind of officer because before the fight you told me you were leading the other soldiers.

Cornelius: I said that?

Hector: You also said you were stationed in Caesarea. So we know quite a bit about you already.

Cornelius: Maybe some of my soldiers can tell me who I am.

Hector: They all went back to Caesarea.

Cornelius: They left me here alone?

Hector: You were hurt. They left you with me because they know I take care of sick people.

Cornelius: Are you a doctor?

Hector: I'm learning to be one.

Cornelius: Do you know enough to make me well?

Hector: Only God can heal that head wound. But

I've cleaned it and bandaged it for you.

Cornelius: I wonder if I have a wife and family who will worry about me?

Hector: Surely your soldiers will tell them what happened.

Cornelius: I hope so. Tell me, what is Ceasarea like?

Hector: Dear me. You don't even remember that?

Cornelius: No.

Hector: Well, it's a lovely town, right along the Mediterranean Sea. It's north of Joppa, and it's near the northern border of Judea.

Cornelius: Joppa. That name rings a bell. I wonder why.

Hector: Joppa? Well, it's a port city on the Mediterannean.

Cornelius: Joppa, Joppa. I'm beginning to remember something. Someone from Joppa came to help me once.

Hector: That's very good. If you can remember who and why, then maybe the rest of your memory will return.

Cornelius: Joppa. My memory has something to do with a vision.

Hector: A vision?

Cornelius: Yes. Now it's beginning to come back. I was praying in my house one day, and an angel appeared to me.

Hector: An angel? Let me feel your head. Your temperature may be rising. I think you're hallucinating.

Cornelius: No, no. My head is quite cool. I really am remembering.

Hector: But such strange memories! You don't have visions and see angels every day, do you?

Cornelius: Of course not! Do you think I'm crazy?! This was very special. That must be why I remember it.

Hector: All right. What do you remember?

Cornelius: I just remember this angel coming to me while I was praying.

Hector: Did it speak to you?

Cornelius: Yes, it said, it said, uh, it said something about Joppa.

Hector: Joppa?

Cornelius: Yes. Now, I remember. The angel told me to send for Simon Peter, a Jew who was staying with Simon the tanner in Joppa.

Hector: Did you know this Simon Peter?

Cornelius: No.

Hector: What a strange message.

Cornelius: The angel told me Peter would answer some questions I had, and would tell me what to do.

Hector: You had questions?

Cornelius: Yes. Oh, I remember this very clearly now. I had questions about God and about what I should believe.

Hector: I thought you Roman soldiers had your own gods and goddesses.

Cornelius: They never seemed right to me somehow. I always felt I was missing something.

Hector: And did you get your answers?

Cornelius: Yes. It's all coming back now. I sent two of my servants and one of my soldiers to Joppa to get this man Peter.

Hector: Did they find him?

Cornelius: Yes, they did. He told them he just had a vision too, and that God told him it was okay for him to go with my servants, even though they weren't Jews.

Hector: Jews don't like to be with other races of people, do they? It's against their religion.

Cornelius: They have their beliefs, but God

showed Peter it was okay to share his faith with people who aren't Jews.

Hector: You have remembered so much. Do you remember your name yet?

Cornelius: It's on the tip of my tongue, but I can't get it out.

Hector: If we talk about what you do remember, maybe your name will come back to you.

Cornelius: Okay.

Hector: Did Peter come to your house?

Cornelius: Yes, he came, and when I told him about the angel, he told me all about Jesus Christ, the Son of the one, true God. When I heard his message, I knew that Jesus was the One I had been searching for all my life.

Hector: What's so special about Jesus?

Cornelius: Peter said the Jews killed Him, but God raised Him from the dead on the third day, and now He has the power to forgive our sins.

Hector: People can make all sorts of claims. How do you know all this is true?

Cornelius: After Peter taught us, a very unusual thing happened. Everyone in my house began to praise God in a language we didn't speak before.

Hector: That does sound strange. Is that some kind of Jewish custom?

Cornelius: Peter said we had received the gift of the Holy Spirit. And because God had given us this gift, Peter realized non-Jews were acceptable to God and we should be baptized.

Hector: But I thought only Jews were baptized.

Cornelius: Peter said God told him Gentiles could be baptized too. That's what he learned in the vision he had before my messengers reached him in Joppa.

Hector: So God prepared Peter to visit you?

Cornelius: Yes.

Hector: He sounds like a very wonderful God.

Cornelius: He is the *only*, true God. And Jesus is His Son.

Hector: You remember all this, but you still can't remember your name.

Cornelius: I'm remembering more and more all the time. I can even see the inside of my house. And I can hear my wife calling my name when I come home from work.

Hector: What does she say?

Cornelius: She says, "Hello, Cornelius."

Hector: Cornelius?

Cornelius: Yes! Cornelius! That's my name. Cornelius! I remember!

Hector: Do you remember how to get home?

Cornelius: Yes, I remember everything now. Except for one thing.

Hector: What's that?

Cornelius: Did we win the fight against the mobsters?

Hector: Yes, they fled. They weren't well organized. They didn't have a chance against your trained soldiers.

Cornelius: I have good men in my command. We train hard every day.

Hector: Well, soldier, I think you're ready to go home.

Cornelius: Thanks for your help. God bless you.

Hector: Good-bye, Cornelius. Take care of yourself.

(*Cornelius exits.*)

Hector: I think I will go to Joppa and find Peter. I want to know more about this Jesus that Cornelius was talking about.

(*Hector exits.*)

I Do Windows

Characters: Raymond
Angie

Raymond: Want to play in the park, Angie?

Angie: I can't. I have to clean my room.

Raymond: Oh, I forgot. I have to clean mine, too.

Angie: Hurry, and maybe we'll have time to play.

Raymond: I need someone to help me clean my room.

Angie: Don't look at me! You're the one who made your room such a mess.

Raymond: What I need is a maid; a personal servant just for me.

Angie: Me too!

Raymond: But I don't know any maids.

Angie: I know one! She's in the Bible.

Raymond: Was she a good maid?

Angie: She was the best. Know who she was?

Raymond: Not yet. Tell me something about her.

Angie: The Bible doesn't tell us what her name was, only who she worked for.

Raymond: I suppose that's who you want me to guess.

Angie: Right. I'll give you a hint. Her master was a Syrian.

Raymond: Oh, that's a big help!

Angie: The Syrians had gone to Israel and captured some people. They took them back to Syria and made slaves out of them.

Raymond: What an awful thing to do!

Angie: This girl was one of the captured ones. She became the personal servant to the wife of a very well-known captain in the Syrian army. He was respected for his successes in battle. But he had a problem.

Raymond: His wife was a sloppy housekeeper.

Angie: No, he had leprosy.

Raymond: Yuck!

Angie: The servant told her mistress that if her husband went to see Elisha the prophet in Samaria, Elisha would heal him.

Raymond: Did the lady and her husband believe the servant?

Angie: I guess so, because the captain asked his king for permission to go to Israel. The king said okay, and gave him a note to take to the king of Israel.

Raymond: What did the note say?

Angie: The note said that the king of Syria was sending his captain to Israel so he could be healed of leprosy.

Raymond: What happened then?

Angie: When the king of Israel read the note, he got upset.

Raymond: How come? I thought it was a pretty nice note.

Angie: The king said, "I can't heal anyone! The king of Syria is trying to pick a fight with me!"

Raymond: Sounds like big trouble.

Angie: Elisha heard about the situation and told the king to send the captain to him.

Raymond: Did he go?

Angie: Yeah. But when the captain got to Elisha's house, Elisha wouldn't see him. Instead, he sent his messenger to talk to him.

Raymond: Why? What did the messenger say?

Angie: He told the captain to dip himself in the Jordan River seven times, and then he would be healed.

Raymond: What a funny way to heal someone!

Angie: The captain was upset. He knew of many rivers that were bigger and prettier than the Jordan. He didn't want to wade in *that* dirty little river. And besides, Elisha hadn't even come out to see him after the captain traveled all the way from Syria!

Raymond: The captain was kind of proud and bull-headed, wasn't he?

Angie: Yeah. He reminds me of you.

Raymond: Me!? You're the bullheaded one! Sometimes you're so bullheaded I think you're going to sprout horns!

Angie: Hmmph! Anyway, the captain's servants convinced him to follow the prophet's orders. So he waded into the Jordan and dipped seven times.

Raymond: Did he get healed?

Angie: When he came up after the seventh dip, his disease was gone. His skin looked as fresh and clean as a baby's skin.

Raymond: Wow! I'll bet he was glad his wife's servant told her about Elisha!

Angie: I'll bet he was too. Do you know his name yet?

Raymond: It's on the tip of my tongue. I keep thinking of a horse, but I know that's not right.

Angie: A horse is a good clue. The captain's name sounds a little like the noise a horse makes.

Raymond: You mean, "neigh?"

Angie: Right.

Raymond: N*eigh*? Angie, have you totally lost your mind?

Angie: Just remember, he wasn't a horse; he was a *man*.

Raymond: Now I know you've lost your mind!

Angie: He was a man. M*an*. That's part of the clue! As a matter of fact, his name rhymes with yours!

Raymond: Neigh and man?

Angie: Yeah.

Raymond: Neigh. Man. You're getting crazier by the minute.

Angie: Say it faster.

Raymond (*faster*): You're getting crazier by the minute.

Angie: Not that, silly. Say the clues faster!

Raymond: Neigh. Man. Neigh. Man. Neigh. Man. Oh! Naaman!

Angie: Right!

Raymond: The maid was the personal servant of Naaman's wife.

Angie: Correct. She was very faithful to her Syrian masters *and* to her Jewish beliefs.

Raymond: If I were Naaman, I would have given her a big reward.

Angie: The Bible doesn't say what happened to her, but I hope Naaman set her free.

Raymond: Me, too.

Angie: I wish I had a faithful personal servant like her.

Raymond: So do I.

Angie: Someday, if we become millionaires, maybe we can afford one.

Raymond: Dream on!

Angie: Until then, we had better clean up our rooms or we won't have time to play in the park.

Raymond: Yes, ma'am!

Playing Politics

Characters: **Joey**
Linda
Mary

Linda: What a neat costume party! I'm so glad I came!

Mary: Me, too! I'm glad our Sunday-school teacher decided to have this party.

Linda: It's fun to dress up like the Bible characters we've been studying all year!

Mary: I love your costume.

Linda: Thanks. Can you guess who I am?

Mary: Mary Magdalene.

Linda: You're right.

Mary: Know who I am?

Linda: You look like Delilah, Samson's wife.

Mary: That's me, all right. See that boy over there? The one dressed up like a king?

Linda: Yes. I wonder who he is.

Mary: I don't know. Let's find out.

Linda: Okay. (*Joey enters.*) Hey, you over there with the crown on your head, who are you?

Joey: This isn't exactly a crown. Guess who I am.

Mary: You're Herod.

Joey: No.

Linda: Then you must be Pharaoh.

Joey: No.

Mary: Who, then?

Joey: I'm a politician.

Linda: A politician! We didn't study any politicians in the Bible.

Joey: Yes, we did.

Mary: We did not.

Joey: Yes, we did.

Linda: Did not.

Mary: What do you mean by a politician? Was he elected like our politicians today are?

Joey: Well, no. But he was a government official in charge of lots of things, so that makes him a politician.

Linda: It does not.

Joey: Does too.

Mary: Does not.

Joey: Whatever you want to call him, that's who I am. But I'm not going to tell you his name.

Linda: Please?

Mary: Yes, please?

Joey: No, you'll have to guess.

Linda: Were you a good politician?

Joey: Very good.

Mary: Did you live in the time of the Old Testament?

Joey: Yes.

Linda: What book are you mentioned in?

Joey: Guess.

Mary: No fair! There are thirty-nine books in the Old Testament! Do you expect us to name all of them?

Joey: No. Just the right one.

Linda: All right, all right. Might as well start at the beginning. Are you in Genesis?

Joey: Yes.

Mary: Hey, that was easy.

Joey: See, you were complaining for nothing.

Linda: Was there something unusual about you?

Joey: Guess.

Mary: Joey, you're making this awfully hard.

Joey: I know. I love it.

Linda: Was there something unusual about the way you looked?

Joey: No.

Mary: About the way you talked?

Joey: No.

Linda: Was there something unusual about your family?

Joey: Sort of.

Mary: Did they all have six toes or something?

Joey: No.

Linda: Give us a better clue.

Mary: Yeah.

Joey: Okay. I had eleven brothers.

Mary: That's not a good clue; lots of people had big families in those days.

Joey: My brothers didn't like me because our father loved me best, and I sort of rubbed it in when I was around them. I'd tell them that I dreamed about them bowing down to me.

Linda: I don't think I would have liked you very well either.

Joey: One day when I came to the fields to visit my brothers, they tied me up and sold me as a slave.

Mary: You had mean brothers.

Joey: I guess I deserved it. I bragged a lot.

Linda: Who did they sell you to?

Joey: Some Midianites who were on their way to Egypt. When we got there, they sold me as a slave.

Mary: So you were a slave first and then a politician?

Joey: Yeah, but before I became a politician, I was a prisoner.

Linda: Who were you a slave for?

Joey: Guess.

Linda: Joey! You're making this too hard!

Mary: Yeah, Joey!

Joey. Okay, okay. I was bought by a man named Potiphar. He was very rich and a fair master, but his wife accused me of a crime I didn't commit. Potiphar believed her and threw me in jail.

Linda: Poor you.

Joey: It was pretty awful; going from my father's favorite son to a slave/prisoner in a foreign country. But, it all turned out okay.

Linda: What happened?

Joey: Well, the pharaoh got mad at his baker and butler and threw them in jail with me. There, they dreamed about some very strange things. When they told me about their dreams, God told me what the dreams meant, and I told them.

Linda: Go on.

Joey: Their dreams came true. Pharaoh hung the baker, but set the butler free.

Mary: So? How did that help you?

Joey: Well, after a while, Pharaoh had some weird dreams too, and his butler told him I could interpret them. So he got me out of prison and told me the dreams.

Linda: Did you know what they meant?

Joey: Yes, God explained them to me. Pharaoh's dreams meant that Egypt would have seven years with good crops and lots of food, and then seven years of famine.

Mary: I think I know your name.

Linda: I don't.

Joey: Whisper it to me. (*Mary whispers in Joey's ear.*) That's right.

Linda: Well, who are you?

Mary: Guess.

Linda: No fair!

Joey: Come on, we'll give you clues.

Linda (*pointing to audience*): I think I'll ask the people out there who you are.

Joey: (*to audience*): Don't tell her!

Linda: (*to audience*): Yes, tell me!

Joey (*to audience*): No!

Mary (*to audience*): Let her guess.

Linda: Then give me some more hints.

Joey: Pharaoh was so impressed with the way I interpreted his dream, that he made me the governor of Egypt. And governors are politicians.

Linda: So, you were your father's favorite son. Then you were a slave, then you were a prisoner, and now you're the governor of Egypt.

Joey: Right.

Linda (*to audience*): Don't tell me his name. Just tell me if you know who he is.

Mary (*to audience*): Don't help her! If she had paid attention in Sunday school, she would know the answer!

Linda: I must have been absent the day you talked about this guy.

Joey: Impossible.

Linda: How come?

Joey: Because you have perfect attendance.

Linda: Oh. Well, maybe I . . . .

Mary: Maybe you fell asleep.

Linda: Oh, hush.

Joey: So who am I?

Linda: I don't know. Give me some more clues.

Joey: I did a real good job of storing grain and other food during the seven years of good harvests. When the famine came, there was enough food for everyone to eat, even for people who didn't live in Egypt. In fact, my brothers came to Egypt to ask for grain.

Mary: And they didn't know he was their long-lost brother.

Joey: That's right; they thought I was dead. But I recognized them right away. I played a few tricks on them and scared them a little bit. Then, after a while, I told them who I was.

Linda: I wish you would tell me who you are.

Joey: I'll give you one, last, big hint.

Linda: Good!

Joey: I had the same name as the man Jesus' mother married.

Linda: You mean Joseph?

Mary: Right!

Linda: Joseph?

Mary: Yes, Joseph.

Linda (*to the audience*): Do you know who they're talking about?

Mary: Keep them out of this. You're the one who's supposed to give the answer.

Joey: Jacob was my father.

Linda: Oh! Now I know! You're *Joseph*, the boy with the coat of many colors!

Joey: That's me.

Linda: And you had two sons named Ephraim and Manassah.

Mary: That's right.

Linda: And the twelve tribes of Israel were named after your brothers and your two sons.

Joey: Right!

Linda: See, I was listening in Sunday school. I just had a mental block, that's all.

Mary: A mental block?

Linda: Yeah, you know. I knew his name, I just couldn't say it.

Mary: Sure.

Linda: Well, it's true.

Joey: Stop arguing, and let's go find out who some of these other characters are.

Linda: Okay.

Mary: Let's go.

Under the Big Top

Characters: **Raymond**
Angie

Angie: I'm going to camp out in the backyard tonight. Will you help me put up the tent?

Raymond: Sure. It's easy.

Angie: I don't think it's easy; there are lots of ropes, and you have to pound stakes into the ground, and the canvas keeps falling on top of me.

Raymond: I'm an expert tent putter-upper. Don't worry.

Angie: Tentmakers have been around for so long they should have figured out an easy way to put tents up.

Raymond: They have. You just don't know it.

Angie: Be quiet, you know-it-all!

Raymond: I can put up a tent so easily you would think I invented tent making.

Angie: Do you know any tentmakers?

Raymond: No.

Angie: Well, I do.

Raymond: You do not.

Angie: I do too. They're mentioned in the Bible.

Raymond: They are?

Angie: See if you can guess the names of three famous tentmakers.

Raymond: All right, but you'd better give me some good clues.

Angie: They're in the New Testament.

Raymond: Good grief, some clue!

Angie: Here's a big clue.

Raymond: I'm waiting.

Angie: A big, big clue.

Raymond: I'm still waiting.

Angie: A big, big, *big* clue.

Raymond: Would you cut it out and get to the clue?

Angie: Okay, okay. They were all teachers of the gospel.

Raymond: Did they use tents for revival meetings like some people do today?

Angie: No. They used to meet in people's houses.

Raymond: Then what did they use the tents for?

Angie: To make money.

Raymond: Huh?

Angie: Making tents is what they did for a living.

Raymond: I'll bet I'd be good at that.

Angie: So far, you aren't very good at guessing who the tentmakers were.

Raymond: Keep sending me big, big clues.

Angie: One of the tentmakers was a great missionary who traveled a lot telling people about Jesus.

Raymond: Oh, that must have been Paul.

Angie: Right. He thought it wasn't right for churches to support him, so he had a job on top of his missionary work. Now, who were the other two?

Raymond: Give me some more clues.

Angie: They were married to each other.

Raymond: Big deal.

Angie: The man was a Jew from Pontus.

Raymond: Pontus?

Angie: Yes. That's an Asiatic province.

Raymond: No kidding.

Angie: The Bible doesn't say where the woman was from.

Raymond: That's a pretty lousy clue if you ask me.

Angie: I didn't ask you. They lived in Rome until Emperor Claudius ordered all Jews to leave the city.

Raymond: I'd hate to have to leave a place just because the ruler didn't want people of my nationality around.

Angie: They moved to Corinth in Greece. That's where Paul met them.

Raymond: Paul knew this couple?

Angie: Yes. He stayed with them, and they made tents together.

Raymond: Business partners, huh?

Angie: When Paul went to Ephesus to preach, the couple went with him.

Raymond: They must have gotten along real well to do that.

Angie: They did. They even helped Paul spread the gospel. In Ephesus, the couple met Apollos, the great speaker and teacher. There were a lot of things he didn't know about the gospel, so they taught him what he needed to know.

Raymond: They must have been pretty smart.

Angie: They were. Are you smart enough to figure out who they were?

Raymond: Of course, if you'll give me another clue.

Angie: Let's see. This couple had church meetings in their home. Later, they moved back to Rome for a while and opened their home for church services again. Paul wrote greetings to them a couple of times in his letters.

Raymond: This is really a hard one. Can't you give me some better clues?

Angie: I'm trying to. Here's one that might help. Four out of six times they are mentioned in the Bible, the woman's name comes first.

Raymond: I wonder why? Did she talk so much her husband couldn't get a word in edgewise?

Angie: No. But maybe she was more involved in spreading the Gospel than he was.

Raymond: Whatever the reason, I still don't know who you're talking about.

Angie: Maybe this clue will be the one you need. The man's name reminds me of an old feather pen.

Raymond: You mean a quill pen?

Angie: Yes.

Raymond: A quill pen. A quill pen. I don't get it.

Angie: Leave off the pen.

Raymond: A quill. A quill. A quill. Oh, of course! Priscilla and Aquila!

Angie: Right!

Raymond: You sure chose a hard one! I had to guess three people.

Angie: You did it, too. Now will you show me how to put this tent up?

Raymond: Sure. It's as easy as saying Priscilla and Aquila.

Personality Plus!

If you find it embarrassing to stand up in front of people but would like to minister to children and adults, puppets may be perfect for you. You can stand behind a stage while the audience sees only the puppet.

Puppets seem to develop a life of their own when they slip over your hand. You can promote this illusion of reality by learning some simple hand movements.

To help make each puppet seem more real, make its mouth open and close as you speak. Close the puppet's mouth on the consonent sounds and open it on the vowel sounds. If you use the word, "Mama," for example, you would open the puppet's mouth twice, once for each of the "a" sounds.

To express surprise, open the puppet's mouth wide. To express fear, a wide open mouth accompanied by a quaking motion or a jump backwards will get the point across.

For sorrow or regret, bend the puppet's head forward. Have the puppet speak slowly, with pauses between some of the words.

To express excitement, make the puppet jump up and down. Its arms will automatically flop as you do this, creating a funny look that should make the audience laugh if you don't overdo it.

To express shyness, have the puppet bend its head down, then slowly look up with its head bent a little sideways.

To indicate that your puppet is listening, tip its head a little to one side and have it nod occasionally.

Experiment with different voice levels and patterns of speech—pauses between words, stuttering, rolling "r's," etc. to help create a personality for each puppet. As you work with puppets, you will develop your own unique way of letting them express emotion.

How to Make Puppets

You will need about one hour to make each puppet. The first six items listed will provide enough material for several puppets:

1. A bag of Poly-fil, often used for making pillows and stuffed animals.
2. A bag of art foam.
3. A roll of masking tape.
4. One container of rubber cement. (If you don't have rubber cement, try Elmer's Glue. However, Elmer's Glue does not work as well for gluing cloth to plastic.)
5. Two pieces of felt material, one red, one a dark color such as green, blue, purple or black.
6. Thread, a needle and a pair of scissors.

For *each* puppet you plan to make you will need:

7. One white sock.
8. One square of Fuzzi Fur
9. One pair of eyes with movable pupils.
10. A pair of hands for a large size doll.
11. Two, empty, eight-ounce plastic containers like the type in which butter or margerine often comes. If you don't buy those products by the container, check with people you know; they may have some.
12. One sixteen-ounce cottage cheese container. Or you may use a small bleach bottle, a small commercial fried chicken bucket, or a round oatmeal box, all with the top and bottom cut out.
13. One long sleeved shirt for a twelve-month-old child. This could be purchased at a thrift shop or from someone whose child has outgrown it.

Once you have the materials, proceed with the instructions on page 74.

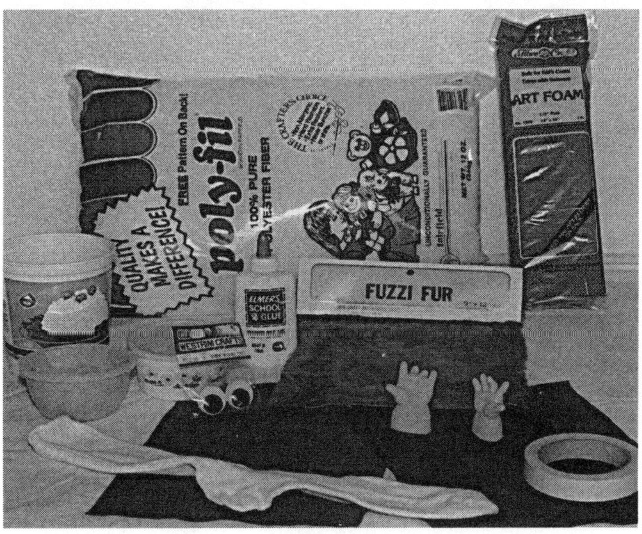

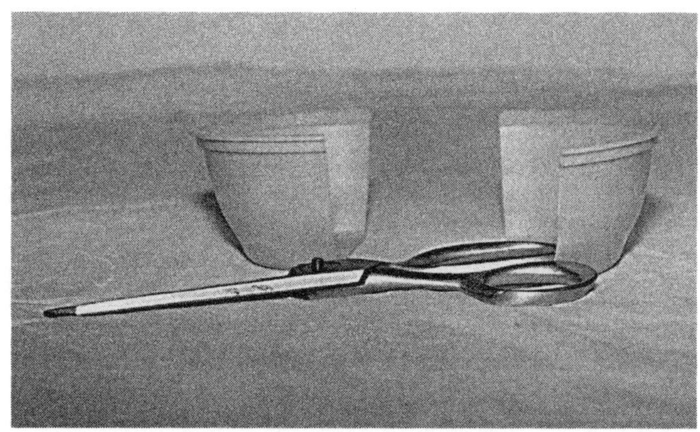

1 Cut one of the eight-ounce plastic containers in half.

2 Glue the lid from one eight-ounce container to one of the container halves. Glue the other side of the lid around half the rim of the uncut eight-ounce container. Reinforce your glue or rubber cement with masking tape.

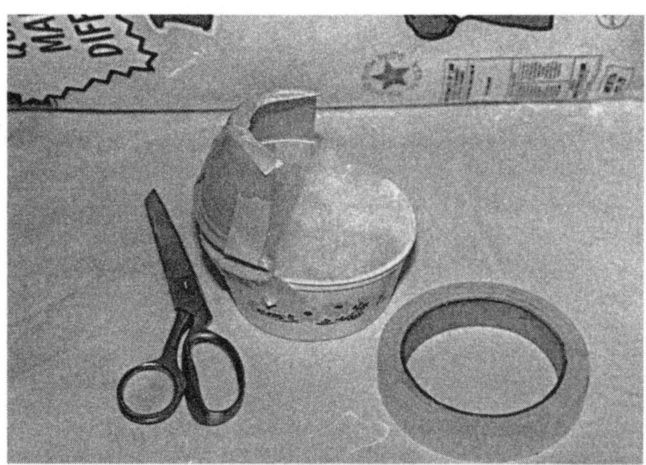

3 Stuff the uncut part of the eight-ounce container with Poly-fil. Line the sharp, cut edge with masking tape.

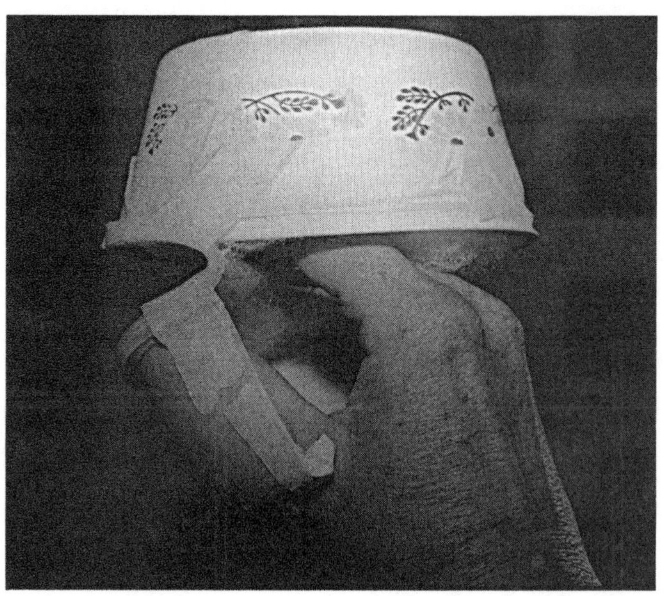

4 Fit your hand into the containers to see if you have the right amount of Poly-fil for a comfortable fit.

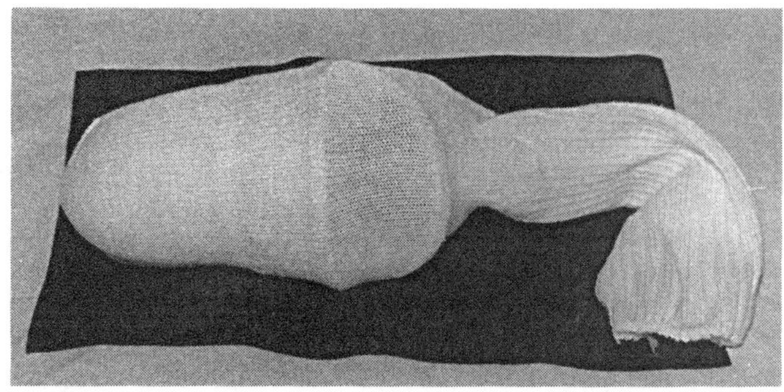

5 Stuff Poly-fil into the end of the white sock to form the forehead. Then slip the partially stuffed sock over the eight-ounce containers that form the puppet's mouth.

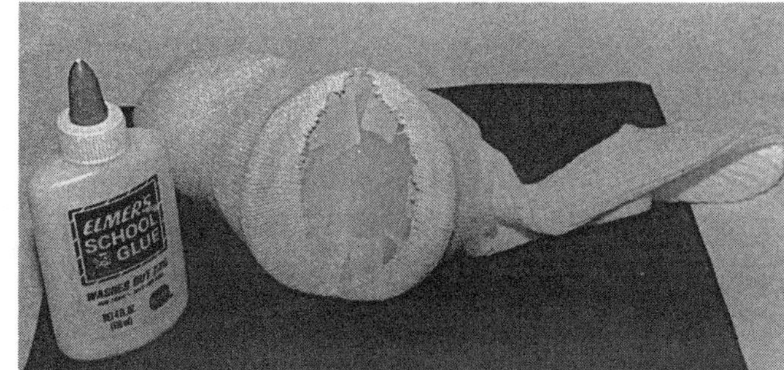

6 Cut the sock where the mouth opens. Using Elmers Glue or rubber cement (which works better), glue the cut edges of the sock to the edge of the plastic lid.

7 Use a lid from an eight-ounce container as a pattern to cut a circle out of the dark-colored felt square.

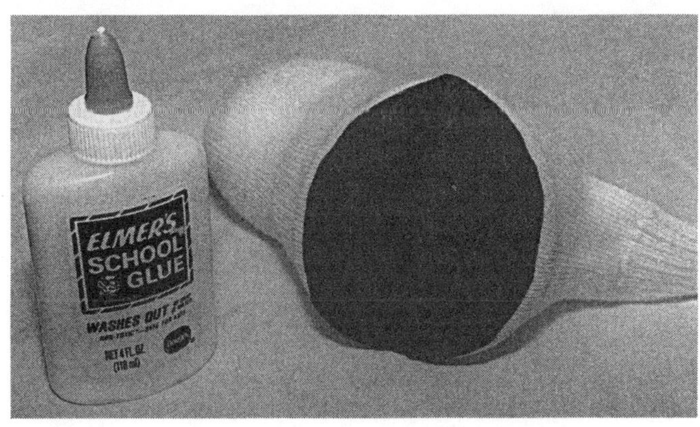

8 Use Elmers Glue or rubber cement to glue the felt circle on the mouth area of the puppet.

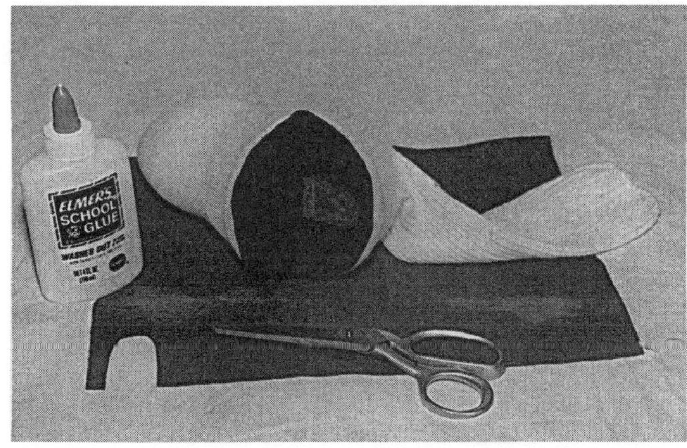

9 Cut a tongue-shaped piece out of the red felt and glue it to the bottom part of the mouth.

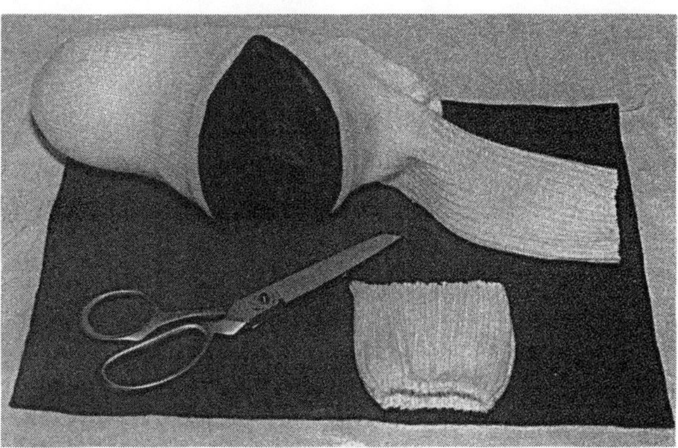

10 Cut off two inches of the sock from the bottom. This piece will form the puppet's nose. (Cut a smaller piece for a smaller nose.)

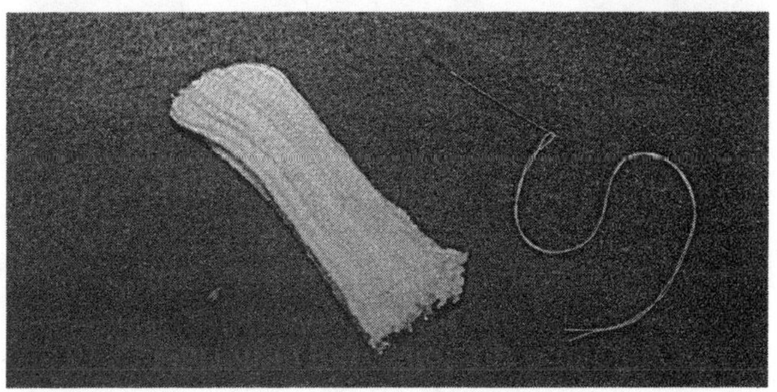

11 Sew the cut off portion of the sock into a long, thin tube. Then turn it inside out so the seam is on the inside.

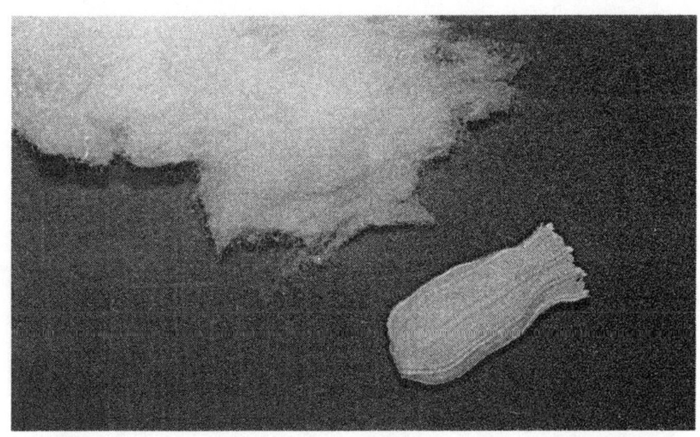

12 Stuff the nose with Poly-fil.

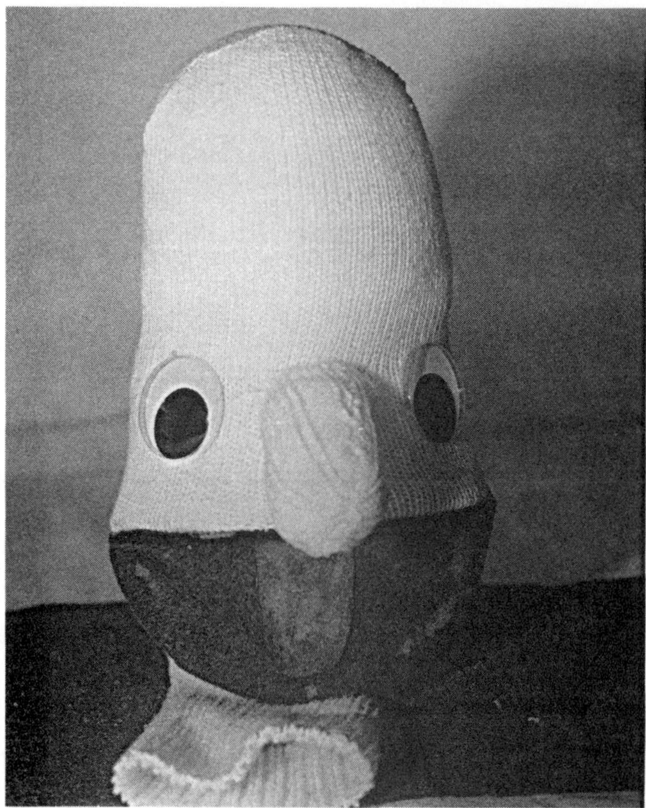

13 Sew the nose onto the puppet about one inch above the mouth.

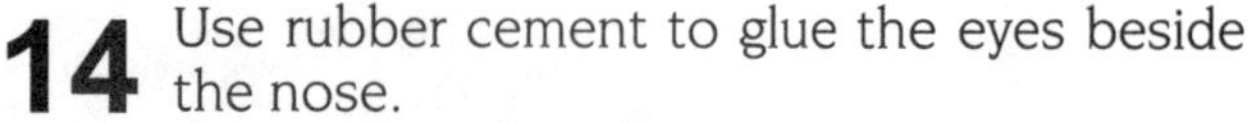

14 Use rubber cement to glue the eyes beside the nose.

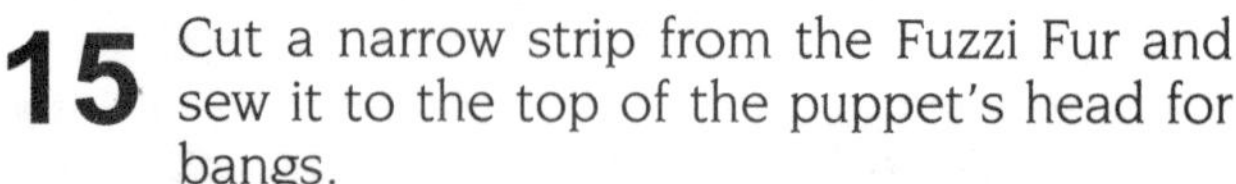

15 Cut a narrow strip from the Fuzzi Fur and sew it to the top of the puppet's head for bangs.

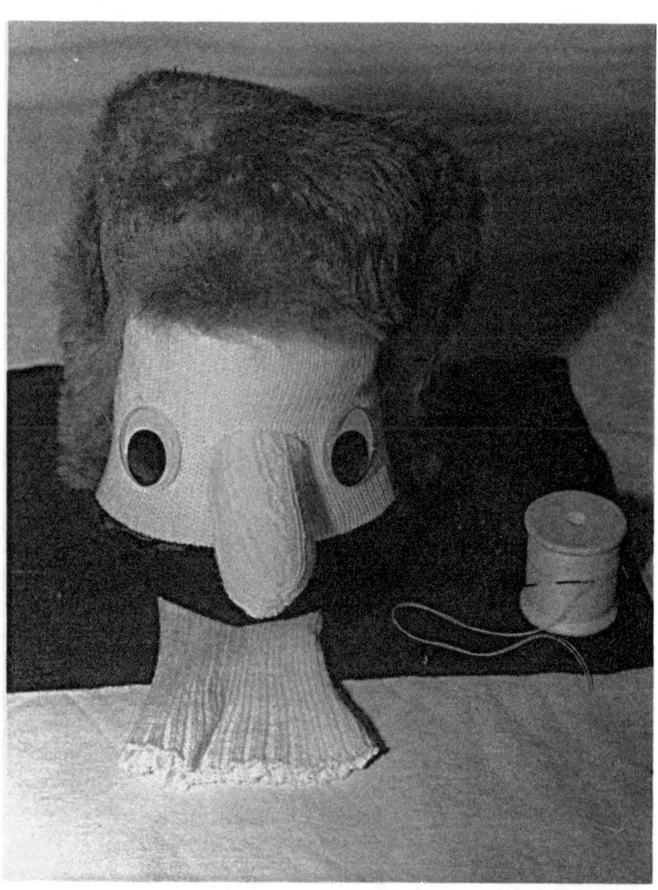

16 Fit the rest of the fur around the puppet's head for hair. Sew it on.

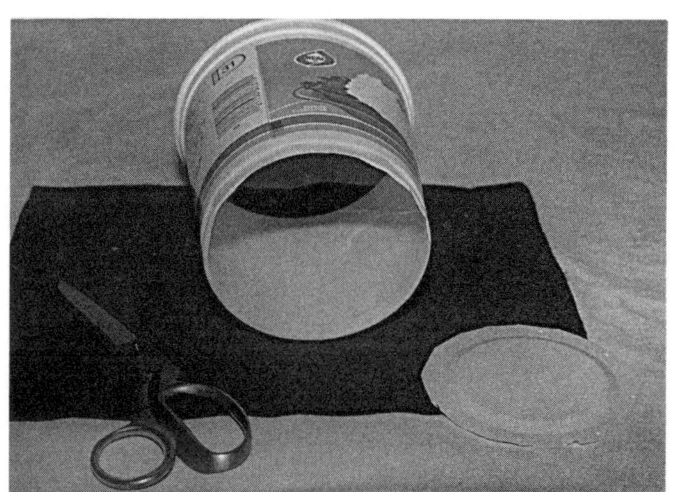

17 Take the round cylinder container and cut out the bottom so your hand will fit all the way through the cylinder.

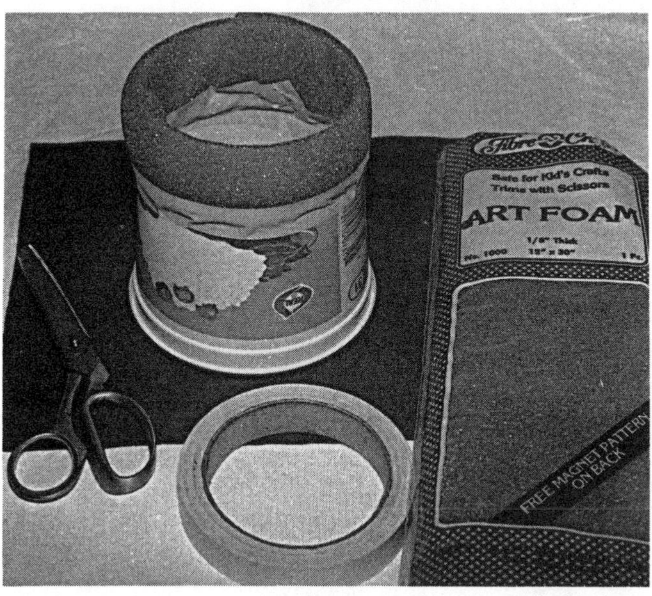

18 Cut a strip of art foam and tape it to the edge you just cut to protect your hand from being scraped. (Lining the inside only will avoid a bulge in the neck.)

19 Slip the sock over the edge of the round cylinder and use rubber cement to glue the sock to the container.

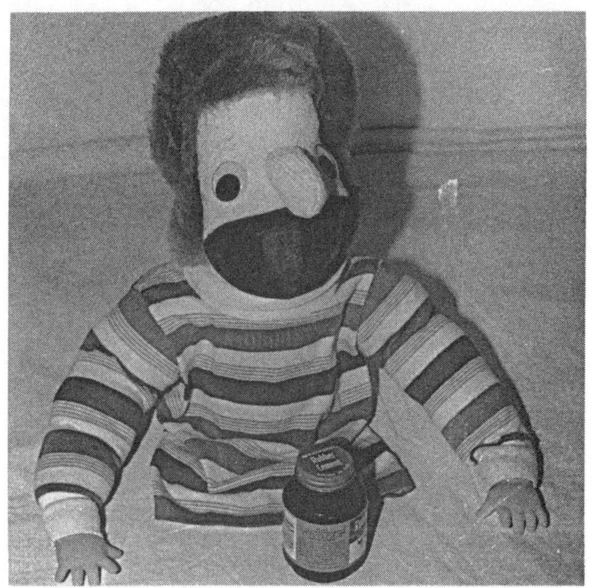

20 Stuff the sleeves of a long-sleeved baby shirt with Poly-fil. (To make the arms look less fat, use a sewing machine to narrow the seams in the sleeves before you stuff them.) Use rubber cement to glue the hands to the sleeves, making sure the thumbs point to the puppet's body. Sew the collar of the shirt to the sock.

21 For a wilder look, such as this puppet has, lightly glue the hair to the puppet's head with Rubber Cement, use frog eyes instead of the flatter eyes, and cut the nose longer.

22 Once you have completed your puppet, set it aside for a few hours so the glue can dry.

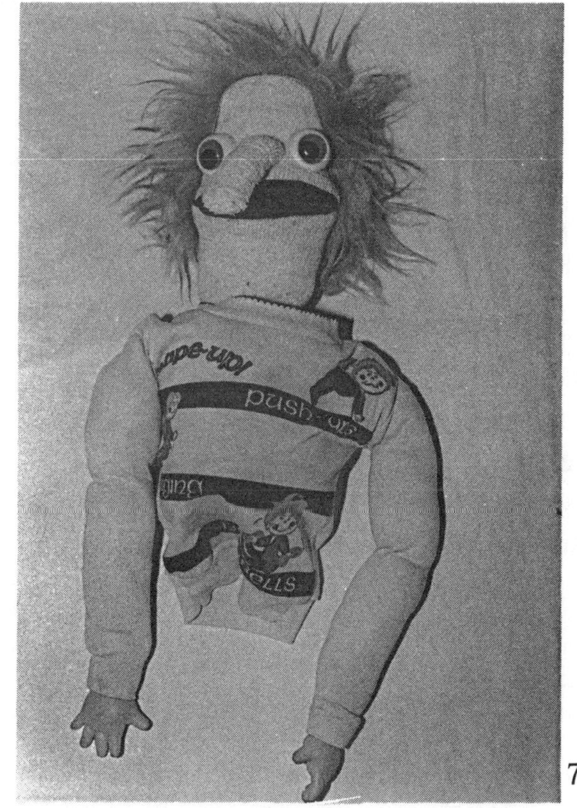

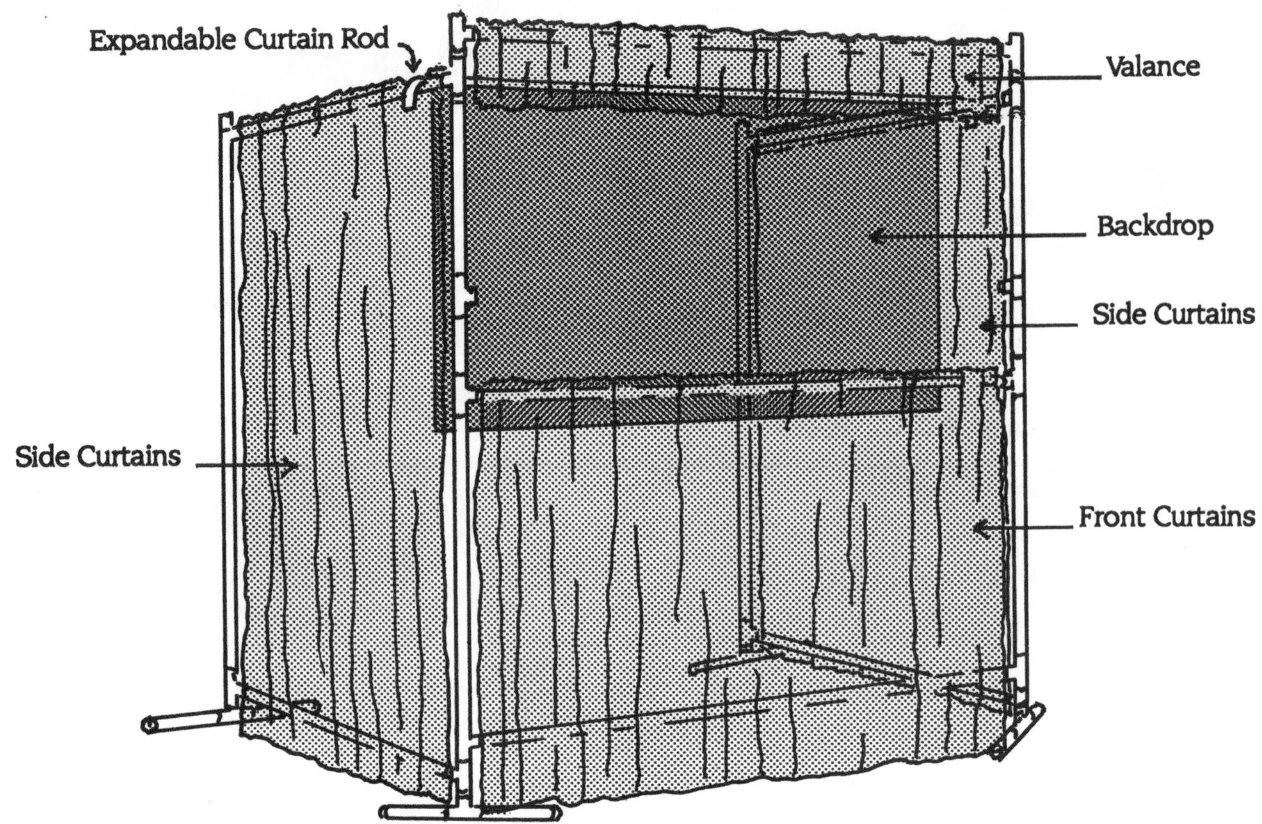

This illustration shows the completed construction with the curtains in place.

How to Build a Puppet Stage

Building a puppet stage isn't hard. The puppet stage shown here can be built any size you want. Use the measurements below to make a stage that is 5 1/2 feet tall, 6 feet wide, and almost 6 feet deep. For a smaller stage, simply reduce the length of the pipe measurements and reduce the yardage of material you will need for curtains.

You will need the following materials:

1. Twenty T's for one-inch PVC pipe. These and other PVS materials called for here can be purchased at most hardware stores.

2. Eight 1-inch PVC caps for the ends of each foot stand.

3. Seven 10-foot lengths of 1-inch PVC pipe.

4. One 3-foot length of 1-inch PVC pipe.

5. Eleven and one half yards of 60-inch wide, dark material for curtains. (Less if you plan to use backdrops of scenery or other colored fabric.)

6. One expandable curtain rod with curved ends. (Must be able to expand to 6-feet without bowing in the center.)

This expandable, curved-end curtain rod (such as is used to hold sheers or kitchen curtains) is used to hold the backdrop for your puppet stage. Since this rod rests freely over the two side top pieces, a backdrop containing appropriate scenery can be easily changed between plays. Backdrop scenery is created for flannelgraph boards and can be purchased for use here from your local Christian bookstore. Or, you may choose to use a backdrop made from the same fabric as the rest of your stage curtains, or a contrasting color This backdrop will not slide as the puppets or puppeteers bump it since the rod is resting on the fabric-covered poles that form the stage sides. However, it can be moved forward or back to allow space for the puppets to move freely about the stage.

The very top rod of the stage may be covered with a short valance to match all the curtains and give your stage a finished, professional appearance. This curtain may be any length you wish (to hide or reveal more or less of the backdrop) but should not interfere with the movements of the puppets. This valance will also hide the backdrop curtain rod. The PVC pipes may be painted to match the curtains.

Cut the 10-foot lengths of PVC pipe as follows:

1. Cut two pipes in half to make four, 5-foot pieces.
2. Cut one pipe into these lengths:
   A. One 5 foot 9 1/2 inch piece.
   B. Three l-foot pieces
   C. One 2 1/2-inch piece. (This piece is for your valance height rod, and is cut from a 14 1/2-inch excess. You may choose to make the valance taller.)
3. Cut a second pipe into the same lengths as in step two.
4. Cut one pipe into these lengths:
   A. One 6-foot piece
   B. One 3-foot piece
   C. One l-foot piece
5. Cut another pipe into the same lengths as in step four.
6. Cut one pipe into these lengths:
   A. Two 22-inch pieces
   B. One 6-foot piece
   C. One 2 1/2-inch piece
7. Cut the three-foot long pipe into these lengths:
   A. Five 2 1/2-inch pieces
   B. Two 9 1/2-inch pieces

Following the diagram, fit each pipe into the T's. Put caps on the legs.

Do not use any form of adhesive. The pipes will fit snuggly enough to form a sturdy, lightweight stage but will be easy to pull apart for storage or for moving from place to place.

To make the curtains, follow these directions:

1. Cut one piece of material 2 1/2 yards long for each side panel. The selvedged edges should be on the sides so you don't have to hem them. Hem the top with a wide enough hem to fit over the five-foot top pipe. Hem the bottom 1/2-inch above the floor.

2. Cut one piece of material 5-feet long for each of two front panels. Seam these two pieces together along one selvedged edge. This will give you 120-inches of fabric to cover a 72-inch pole, so you will have a nice fullness to the front stage curtain. The selvedged edges run along the sides and center seam of this curtain for a clean, finished look. Hem the top so it will fit over the 6-foot pipe and the bottom 1/2-inch from the floor. *This curtain length reaches from the* ***top****, front curtain rod to the floor. If you plan to use the lower rod as well, you will need to make another, adjustable (Velcro?) hem.*

3. Two 3 1/2-foot panels (seamed together) may be used for a matching backdrop. This top hem will have to be wide enough to slide over the curved-corner, expandable rod. The bottom should be hemmed just below the front panel to hide any activity within the stage. If you plan to make a backdrop of a contrasting color or use prepared scenery backfrops, this length of fabric may be eliminated from your purchase.

4. The remaining 2 1/2 feet of fabric may be used for your valance, and may be made whatever length you wish.

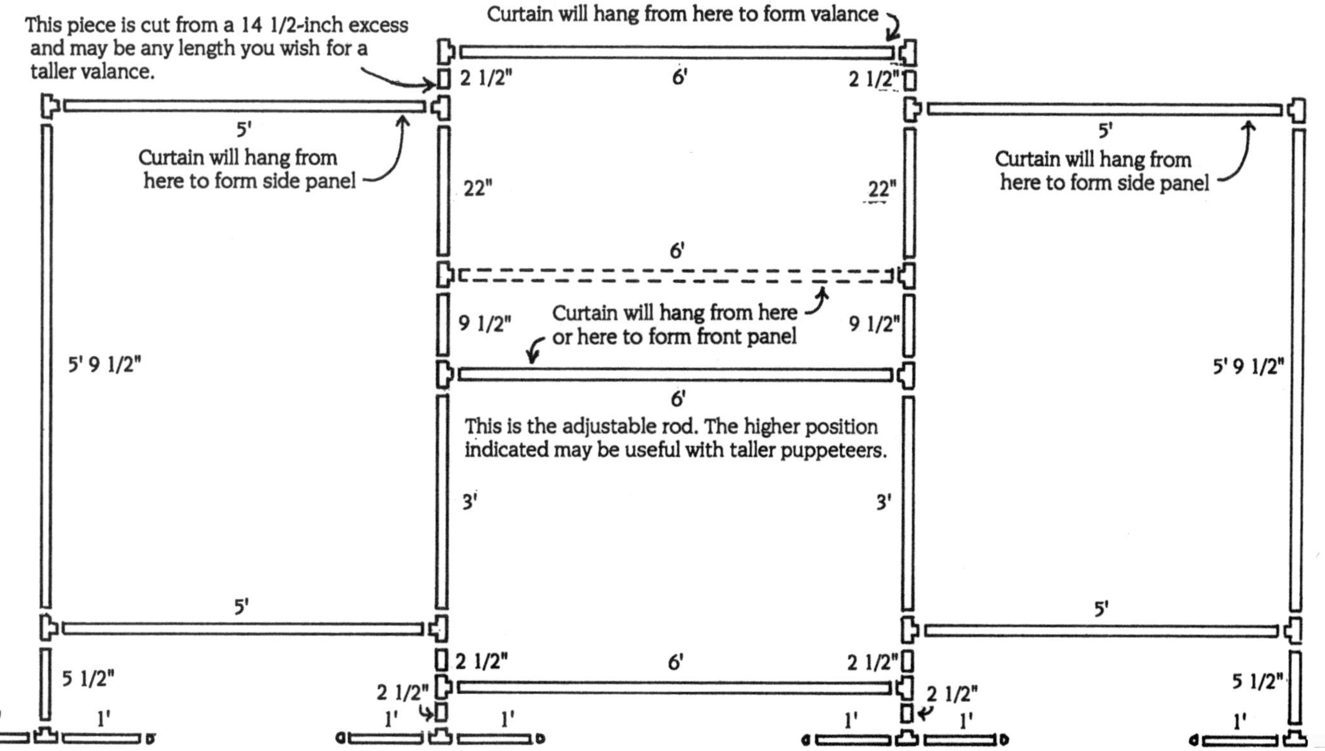